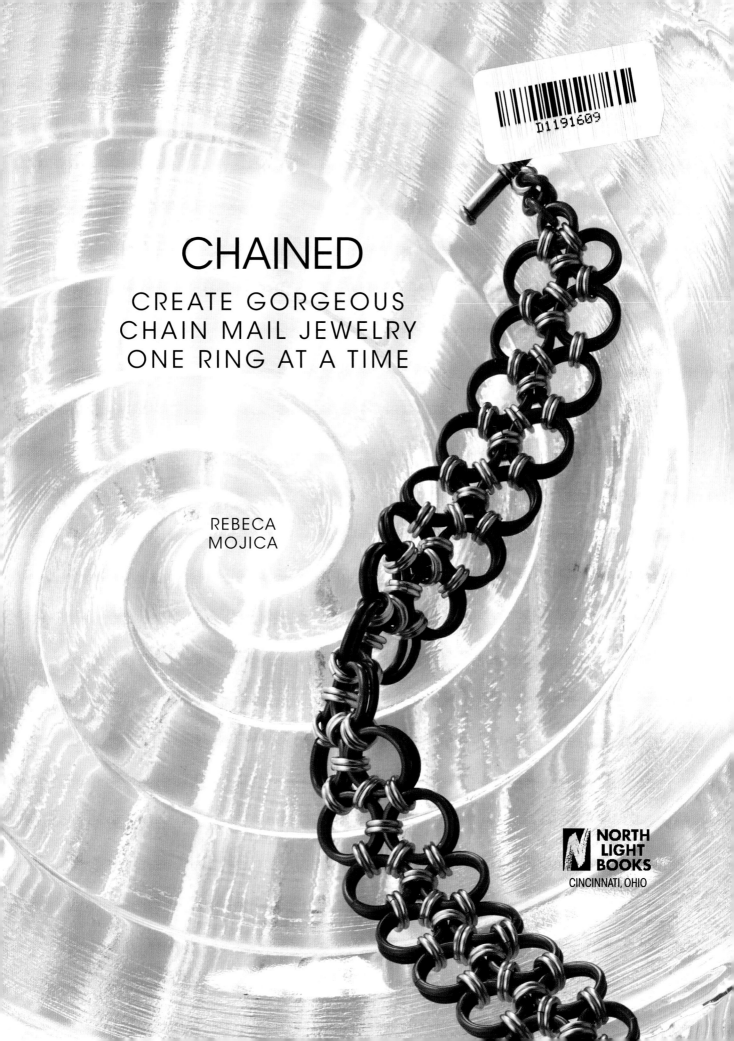

CHAINED

CREATE GORGEOUS CHAIN MAIL JEWELRY ONE RING AT A TIME

REBECA
MOJICA

NORTH LIGHT BOOKS
CINCINNATI, OHIO

www.fwmedia.com

14 13 12 11 10   5 4 3 2 1

DISTRIBUTED IN CANADA BY FRASER DIRECT
100 Armstrong Avenue
Georgetown, ON, Canada L7G 5S4
Tel: (905) 877-4411

DISTRIBUTED IN THE U.K. AND EUROPE BY F+W MEDIA INTERNATIONAL
Brunel House, Newton Abbot, Devon, TQ12 4PU, England
Tel: (+44) 1626 323200, Fax: (+44) 1626 323319
Email: postmaster@davidandcharles.co.uk

DISTRIBUTED IN AUSTRALIA BY CAPRICORN LINK
P.O. Box 704, S. Windsor NSW, 2756 Australia
Tel: (02) 4577-3555

LIBRARY OF CONGRESS CATALOGING IN PUBLICATION DATA
Mojica, Rebeca.
  Chained create gorgeous chain mail jewelry one ring at a time / Rebeca Mojica.
 – 1st ed.
    p. cm.
  Includes index.
  ISBN 978-1-4403-0308-1 (alk. paper)
  1. Jewelry making. 2. Metal-work. 3. Chains (Jewelry) I. Title.
  TT212.M64 2010
  739.27–dc22
                      2010022744

Edited by **Jennifer Claydon**
Designed by **Kelly O'Dell**
Production coordinated by **Greg Nock**
Photography by **Jenna L. Deidel, Ric Deliantoni**
    and **Christine Polomsky**
Illustrations by **Jason Scerena**
Styling by **Lauren Emmerling**
Wardrobe styling by **Megan Strasser**
Makeup by **Nikki Deitsch**

METRIC CONVERSION CHART

To convert	to	multiply by
Inches	Centimeters	2.54
Centimeters	Inches	0.4
Feet	Centimeters	30.5
Centimeters	Feet	0.03
Yards	Meters	0.9
Meters	Yards	1.1

DEDICATION
For Dinner Group

ACKNOWLEDGMENTS
Thanks to:

Jenna Deidel, for spending countless hours in a tiny, hot photography room, painstakingly shooting the step-by-step photos for this book and staying in good humor despite the less-than-ideal shooting conditions; Kat Wisniewski, for keeping the studio running smoothly while I holed myself up to write, for the weekly manicures that kept my fingers in tip-top shape, and for "proofmailling" several of the finished pieces; Vanessa Walilko for proofreading, weaving some of the pieces in this book and sanity-checking the ring sizes for the projects; Jason Scerena for anodizing thousands of niobium rings; Jen Hohe for coordinating my project needs with the production schedule of our ring makers; Emily Fiks for all her hard work in the studio gathering rings for book projects and classes; Sky Cubacub, Carrie Evenowski, Angelique Gall, Jennifer Hyatt, Christa Krasneck, L. Lindsey, Laura Moore, Oksana Movchan and Andrew Zablocki for testing most of the patterns you see in this book as well as dozens more that didn't make the final cut; my editor Jenni, for patiently and thoroughly answering all my questions; all the students and customers of Blue Buddha Boutique, without whom I would not have had a reason, nor the inspiration, to write this book; artisans Spider, Lord Charles, Zlosk and Maillemaster for encouraging me to follow my passion; metalsmiths Sarah Chapman and Kathy Frey for openness in sharing jewelry experiences, knowledge and resources; Caravan Beads for giving me the opportunity to begin teaching maille; my mom Rita Mojica for her enthusiastic support; Rach@el Bild, for being there from the beginning; Ben Evans for his love, support and feedback; Kaplan Test Prep for taking my teaching abilities to the next level; Aerosmith for providing an excellent soundtrack for mailling; and finally to Zed the cat for reminding me to relax and have fun along the way.

ABOUT THE AUTHOR

Rebeca Mojica is an award-winning chainmaille artist and instructor. By using colorful rings and combining classic weaves in new ways, she has redefined this ancient craft. At current count, this self-taught artist knows over one hundred weaves, including more than a dozen patterns of her own creation.

Rebeca has been teaching maille for almost as long as she has been making it. She helps students discover that they, too, can create beauty using only their hands, pliers and jump rings.

When she had difficulty finding high-quality supplies for her designs, Rebeca decided to found Blue Buddha Boutique in 2003 with a focus on precision sizing and clean, polished rings. Originally operated out of a spare bedroom in her home, the company is now one of the largest chainmaille suppliers in the world, shipping orders to all fifty states in the U.S. and more than thirty countries.

Rebeca is considered a pioneer and one of the industry's only experts. She teaches regularly at local bead stores and art centers, and has taught at the international Bead&Button Show. She has also been a guest instructor for the Fashion Department at the School of the Art Institute of Chicago. Her instructional projects have been published in multiple books and magazines.

Rebeca's necklace *Poseidon's Embrace*, made of 14,500 titanium and stainless steel jump rings, won 3rd place in the Finished Jewelry category of the Bead Dreams 2009 competition.

Rebeca is a member of the Chicago Craft Mafia and Chicago Metal Arts Guild. She is a contributing editor to *Step by Step Wire Jewelry* magazine. Her work has appeared on CLTV and in the *Chicago Tribune* and *The New York Times*.

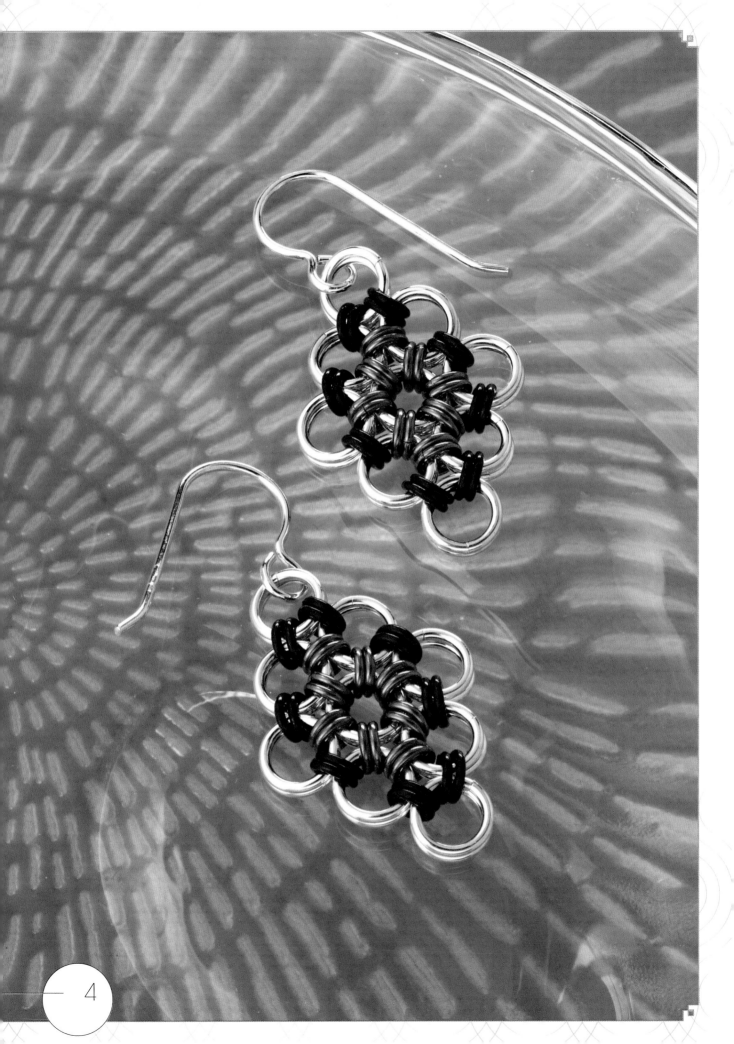

Table of Contents

Welcome to the World of Chain Mail!

While at a Renaissance Faire in Germany, I saw several people wearing gypsy-style chain mail belts with dramatically draped chains and beads. I had to have one! Unfortunately— or in retrospect, perhaps at the most serendipitous turning point of my life—none of the Faire vendors were selling chain mail. I found one or two belts on the Internet, but nothing quite like what I envisioned. What I did find was "1,000+ jump rings—make your own chain mail!" Having made jewelry at summer camp, I figured I would give it a go. However, once the rings arrived, I had no idea what to do with them, so they sat untouched for several weeks.

On May 4, 2002, I finally opened the package. My life would never be the same.

The rings were 16 gauge galvanized steel, which is one of the hardest metals to work with. I only had huge pliers from my toolbox, and my scrawny arms struggled to get the tools to obey. Somehow, though, after four hours of hard work—plus a little bit of cursing, a drop of blood, and yes, even a piece of flying chain mail tossed in a moment of ultimate frustration—a belt emerged. It wasn't a masterpiece, and the clasp point left a little something to be desired. Nonetheless, I was thrilled. I would later find out that what I'd done was called European 4-in-1, commonly seen in armor shirts.

I had enough jump rings left over to make another belt, which turned out fancier than the first. A small pile of rings remained, and from these I created something that should have been the Box weave. (Once I actually learned what Box was, it was pretty clear that my myriad of mistakes in a vaguely rectangular shape was, well, not Box at all.)

I have always been a tactile person, so it is not surprising that I was drawn to the ancient art of chain mail. As I worked my way through my first bag of rings, I discovered how soothing it felt to link together ring after ring and watch a pattern unfold. I couldn't wait to make more. In other words, I was completely, hopelessly addicted!

The addiction has only grown with time. I chain mailed every single day for the next three years.

Even today, I link rings at least five or six days a week. I appreciate how each piece comes alive in my fingers—the different textures all yield unique personalities. I couldn't pick a single favorite weave if I tried.

People often say to me, "You must have so much patience." But when you do something you love, patience doesn't even enter the picture. This truly is my passion, my love. I am excited that this book has given me the opportunity to share something so close to my heart, and I sincerely hope you enjoy creating mail as much as I do.

You'll find more technique instruction in *Chained* than in any other book on this subject. Through more than 1,000 hours of teaching, I've learned the common stumbling blocks and questions students have. I've included the tips and tricks I've acquired over the years to help you save time and avoid frustration. I'll help you navigate the confusing world of ring sizes with conversions between metric and imperial measurements. I can't completely tear down the mathematical barriers surrounding chain mail, but I've tried to at least provide ladders and loopholes to those needing them.

Technically, this book contains more than twenty patterns plus many variations, but I'd rather you think of it as a doorway to an infinite number of patterns, a celebration of diversity. The creative chain mail artist is analogous to a master chef—using a recipe only as a base from which to experiment with different flavors (metals), colors and textures.

I hope that by showing you how easy it is to manipulate jump ring patterns to customize your pieces, your chain mail spark will be ignited. Erase your preconceived notions of this ancient craft and join me in pushing the boundaries of what is considered chain mail.

Welcome to the addiction!

—*Rebeca*

P.S. If you're already addicted, well … what can I say? I knew we'd find each other someday.

Starting Out

Whether you've been making chain for ten years, or have yet to weave your first piece, you'll find this first chapter to be bursting at the seams with useful information.

I'm sure you're eager to get started with projects, but I want to make sure you are familiar with the terms, techniques and tools that we'll be using throughout this book. I encourage you to at least skim this chapter for now, flagging sections that you'll want to reference later.

In the first few pages, you'll find a bit of historical information, along with a listing of highly respected resources (should you wish to find out more about the origins of this craft). We then move on to a brief overview of how jump rings are made and detailed descriptions of commonly used metals. Other sections guide you through ring measurements, tools used for weaving, how to finish and embellish your pieces, basic wire techniques and finally, how to care for your jewelry.

Lest you flip to the ring measurements explanation and find your heart sinking at the sight of all the charts, fear not! You do not need to fully understand every nuance in order to get started, as conversions are listed for each project. For those wishing to take their designs to the next level, it is critical to have a good grasp on measurements. New chain mailers, however, can just concentrate on using the sizes as listed, without worrying about all the math behind the weaves.

The bulk of this chapter covers techniques for opening and closing your jump rings, beginning on page 20, and a few quick ways to add beads to your chain mail projects. You'll also find several pages of troubleshooting. This information is very important, because these techniques can be difficult to master on your own. Even veteran weavers will discover a few tips and tricks to make your mailing easier and faster.

Just before you're ready to start tackling the jewelry projects, pay particular attention to How to Use this Book on pages 36–37. I've written the instructions in a very specific way, using certain symbols and terms over and over again. Once you understand the formula, you can make the most out of the instructions and progress smoothly from project to project.

Happy weaving!

History of Chain Mail

Chain mail (also known as chainmaille, or simply maille) is typically armor or jewelry made by connecting metal rings to one another. The word maille derives from the French word *maille* (mesh), which comes from the Latin word *macula* (mesh of a net). It is because of this etymology that I, like many other chain mail artists (or "maillers"), prefer to spell chainmaille with an "le" at the end, as opposed to using the media-approved spelling of "chain mail." Well, that, and to distinguish our beloved craft from chain letters!

Chain mail is one of the earliest forms of metal armor. It is believed that the Celts invented mail armor sometime in the late first millennium B.C. The oldest pieces of complete mail armor, discovered in the graves of Celtic warriors, are more than 2,700 years old. Other evidence of mail fragments, which likely were decorative elements, has been found in graves from the fifth century B.C. in the Iberian Peninsula and Scythia (an area between Europe and Asia). Although most historical chain mail is armor, linked-metal jewelry techniques were also used by cultures as diverse as the Vikings and the ancient Egyptians. It is difficult to trace the history of chain mail, because much of the "evidence" was destroyed in battle or over time. Many pieces that survive today may have been high-quality pieces passed on from generation to generation. Other pieces are certainly not royal heirlooms and could even have been stolen from a corpse after a battle. If you are interested in historical chain mail,

I recommend that you visit the website of The Mail Research Society (www.themailresearchsociety. erikds.com).

Chain mail has experienced a resurgence in recent years. Some artists make armor to use in staged battles or at Renaissance Faires. Others prefer to create chain mail jewelry, and still others make sculptures. The versatility of this medium is astounding; artists have created chessboards, belts, dresses, baskets and even sunglass lenses out of chain mail.

Chain mail can be made from virtually any material that can be formed into a circle. This includes most metals. In recent years, materials such as beads, rubber rings and mini glass donuts have been combined with metal rings to form innovative designs.

The number of known chain mail patterns is impressive: More than 1,000 weaves are documented in the library of Maille Artisans International League. M.A.I.L. is an international community of artisans and volunteers dedicated to the advancement of the chain mail art form. Their library (located on their website, www. mailleartisans.org) includes photos of each pattern and instructions for a wide variety of weaves. Most of these are modifications of basic patterns, but each weave is distinct. Today's chain mail weavers continue to develop new designs and innovative applications for chain mail.

Mail neck defense, 1700s – 1800s
Higgins Armory Museum, Worcester, Massachusetts USA
Japan
Iron
1 lb 5 oz
The detail below shows a small section of Japanese mail, which is highly distinctive and most resembles mail made by the Etruscans of ancient Italy.

How Jump Rings Are Made

Chain mail is composed of tiny metal circles called jump rings. A jump ring is made by taking a length of wire and wrapping it around a rod, known as a mandrel, to make a coil. In metalsmithing classes, students generally do this by hand. Serious chain mail weavers will use an electric setup, either attaching the mandrel to a power screwdriver or drill, or by using jump ring making tools.

Once a coil is made, it is then cut with wire cutters or with a saw. Rings that are cut with wire cutters are often referred to as "pinch-cut" rings, since the ends of the rings are squeezed until they break, thereby creating points on the ends of the ring. Saw-cut rings are preferable for jewelry, as the saw creates a perfect line, known as a kerf, through the metal. This line allows you to close the ring seamlessly.

Some people find it satisfying to create jump rings and have control over the entire chain mail process. There is specific information in other books, and notably on the Internet, on how to make your own jump rings. The organization M.A.I.L. (www.mailleartisans.org) mentioned on the previous page is an excellent resource for this type of information. If you suspect you're one of those people who would love making your own rings, I encourage you to seek out this information and give it a go!

Many people prefer to be "weavers rather than spinners" and simply purchase pre-made jump rings. A decade ago it was difficult to find reliable sources for jump rings, but as chain mail has grown in popularity, many companies have started to offer chain mail supplies (see Recommended Suppliers and Resources on page 142).

Throughout this book, I'll refer to a few measurements with regard to jump rings. The inner diameter and the wire diameter are most important, and we'll discuss these concepts on pages 16–17.

Mail shirt, perhaps 1600s

Higgins Armory Museum, Worcester, Massachusetts USA
India or Persia
Steel; brass
15 lb 11 oz
The shirt at left mainly features robust links with an interior diameter of 7mm. The collar has a very tight weave and tiny links, approximately 4mm interior diameter. There are brass edging links on the collar and skirt and the top edge of the collar is finished with very small solid links.

These tools can be used to make a wide variety of jump rings.

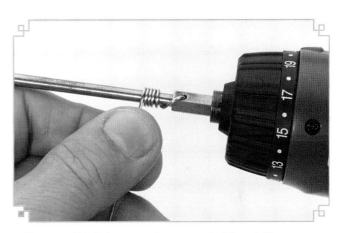

Here, a coil is being created on a mandrel in a drill.

The ring above on the left is pinch-cut, while the ring on the right is saw-cut. As you can see, the saw-cut ring has a cleaner cut.

Metal Facts

There are many different metals to choose from when making chain mail jewelry. Some metals are more suited to particular applications than others. For example, I don't suggest making a belt out of aluminum rings because it won't be strong enough for daily use. Steel, on the other hand, is great for this purpose.

I've divided the metals into base (non-precious) and precious metals. Most of the projects in this book are made using base metals, simply because they are more accessible for a beginning student. However, as much as possible, conversions to the closest precious metal sizes are also listed. The temper and alloys for the metals used in this book are listed for folks who make their own rings.

BASE METALS

BRIGHT ALUMINUM

*recommended metal for beginners

Don't mistake regular aluminum for bright aluminum. Choose bright aluminum or your hands will be covered with black rub-off in a few minutes!

Pros: Inexpensive; smooth and shiny; very easy to work with. It is widely accepted that aluminum is very poorly absorbed through the skin, so metal toxicity is not a concern.

Cons: Not as durable as other metals; smaller gauges (20 and 22) won't hold up to a lot of stress. Although once valued more highly than gold, it doesn't have the prestige of other metals. Some people may notice a faint gray rub-off with bright aluminum (the amount of rub-off may depend on the acid content of your skin; several people who have reactions to copper also react to aluminum). Over time, aluminum will corrode slightly, losing a bit of shine. This process stops once the very thin surface layer has corroded.

Cleaning: Easy to clean if it gets dirty; washing in soapy water will bring back the shine.

Extra Information: Bright aluminum is less weighty than other metals, which you may find to be a pro or con. (Most men and many women want something much more weighty.)

Alloy: 5356; Temper: Full Hard; Composition: aluminum: 92.9–95.3%; magnesium: 0.8–1.2%; possible trace amounts of chromium, copper, iron, silicon, zinc manganese and titanium.

ANODIZED ALUMINUM

*recommended metal for beginners

Aluminum is colored by first anodizing the rings (dipping them in an electrically charged solution) to prepare the surface. They are then dyed. Rings in the same batch may vary drastically in color, or they may be extremely uniform.

Pros: The least expensive of the anodized metals; easy to work with. The only anodized ring to come in certain colors, including red and orange.

Cons: The colors in aluminum will fade with time. The color can be scratched by harder metals, so be careful when weaving and storing your piece. If the dye was not absorbed well, it may begin to flake off at a stress point (generally the part of the ring directly opposite the kerf) when you're working with it. Color varies from dye lot to dye lot.

Cleaning: Oils from skin may change the colors. Some of the color can be restored by washing the piece in soap and water.

Alloy: 5154-H18; Temper: Full Hard; Composition: aluminum: 96.6–98.5%; magnesium: 1.5–2.1%; trace amounts of chromium, copper, iron, manganese, silicon, titanium and zinc.

Tip

Metals are available in different tempers (hardnesses) and alloys. One supplier's steel may not be the same as another's. To be safe, ask the supplier for the exact alloy and for any special care/cleaning requirements.

From left to right: Bright aluminum, anodized aluminum, jewelry brass, bronze, stainless steel, copper, enameled copper, rubber rings

JEWELRY BRASS

*recommended metal for beginners

There are different alloys of brass. Some are more yellow than others. Jewelry brass has a higher copper content than other brass. Some folks use other terms for jewelry brass, such as red brass, red bronze or new gold. However, note that those alloys may be exactly the same, or they may have 2–3 percent more copper.

Pros: Strong, especially in thicker gauges. Weighty.

Cons: Some brass is very soft and unsuitable for chain mail. Alloys that are Half Hard are best, but these are harder to bend in 18 gauge and thicker. Because it is an alloy of copper and zinc, brass patinas very fast.

Cleaning: Use any commercial jewelry cleaner that says it is safe for brass.

Extra Information: Brass develops a patina with age that you may like or dislike. Jewelry brass is heavy, which may be considered a pro or a con.

Alloy: C226; Temper: Half Hard; Composition: copper: 87%; zinc: 13%.

BRONZE

Pros: Highly durable. Weighty. If you want the look of aged copper, but a stronger metal, use bronze, which is an alloy of copper and tin.

Cons: Once again, because this metal contains copper, it develops a patina fast. Can be hard to work with in 18 and 16 gauge.

Cleaning: Use any commercial jewelry cleaner that says it is safe for brass or copper.

Alloy: C150; Temper: Half Hard; Composition: copper: 92% or more; tin: approximately 5%; phosphorus: 0.03–0.35%; trace amounts of lead, iron and zinc.

STAINLESS STEEL

Pros: Highly durable; does not tarnish.

Cons: Can be very difficult to bend in gauges 18 and thicker. You'll need heavy-duty pliers. Saw-cut steel is expensive (because it isn't easy cutting through steel with a saw!). This is not an appropriate metal for beginners, especially 18 and 16 gauge!

Extra Information: Stainless steel is quite weighty, which you may find to be a pro or con.

Alloy: 304; Temper: Half Hard; Composition: iron: approximately 69%; chromium: 19%; nickel: 9.25%; magnesium: approximately 2%; silicon: 1%; carbon: 0.08%; phosphorous: 0.045%; sulfur: 0.03%.

COPPER

*recommended metal for beginners

Pros: Easy to work with, even in this temper.

Cons: Tarnishes quickly. Store jewelry in resealable bags to slow tarnishing. Squeeze out as much of the air from the bag as possible before closing. It is a weak metal, so you must be extra gentle with copper chain mail pieces, especially those with 20 or 22 gauge rings.

Cleaning: Soak in pure lemon juice and salt for a few seconds, then rinse with soapy water.

Extra Information: As with aluminum, most people either love copper or hate it. Some people don't mind the tarnishing, and in fact, many love the range of hues copper displays as it goes through the tarnishing process. Copper is also heavy.

Alloy: C110; Temper: Full Hard; Composition: copper: 99.9%; possible trace elements.

ENAMELED COPPER, INCLUDING ENAMELED SILVERED COPPER

This type of enameled copper has nothing to do with the jewelry technique of copper enameling. The name enameled copper comes from the electrical industry, as this type of wire is used often in transformers and motors. The craft industry uses the same product, just with prettier colors!

Pros: Very easy to work with; comes in many colors. The silvered colors are especially vivid because there is a layer of pure silver underneath the plastic "enameled" coating.

Cons: Very soft. When the plastic coating is added, the metal becomes annealed, so it is soft. The wire is coated before it is cut, so you can sometimes see bits of copper right at the closure.

Alloy: proprietary; Temper: Dead Soft (due to the coating); Composition: coating is a polyurethane and nylon blend.

RUBBER RINGS (SILICONE)

Rings made of rubber are becoming more common in chain mail. They can be substituted for closed rings in many weaves, as long as the sizes are a close match.

Pros: Inexpensive. The silicone rings I use are non-latex rubber, making them easy to clean and usually non-allergenic. They last longer than other types of rubber rings (such as EPDM and neoprene).

Cons: Colors can be inconsistent (same issues with dye lots as anodized aluminum). Over many years, the rubber will dry out and crack.

PRECIOUS METALS

From left to right: Sterling silver, gold-fill, anodized niobium, anodized titanium

STERLING SILVER

Sterling silver differs from fine silver. The addition of copper to silver to form sterling silver strengthens the silver, making it suitable for chain mail. Fine silver is 99 percent silver. Though a purer alloy, fine silver is significantly softer and generally not recommended for chain mail.

Although sterling silver is considered semi-hypoallergenic, some people have allergic reactions to it, probably because of the copper content. These highly sensitive people do better with fine silver, a high karat gold, niobium, titanium or possibly argentium silver, a relatively new alloy of non-tarnishing silver.

Pros: Smooth and shiny; easy to work with; nice weight. And of course, silver has prestige.

Cons: Pricey; thinner gauges can be weak; tarnishes easily. Always make sure your jump rings are made from at least Half Hard wire, never Dead Soft.

Alloy: .925 sterling; Temper: Half Hard; Composition: silver: 92.5%; copper: 7.5%.

GOLD-FILL

Gold-fill is made of a layer of gold surrounding a base metal core, and is generally expressed in fractional numbers (for example, 14/20). The first number refers to how many karats the gold has out of a possible 24 total karats. The second number, 20, means that the gold layer is 5% (1/20) the total thickness of the wire. Although gold is considered semi-hypoallergenic, some people have allergic reactions to gold (generally less than 18k). These highly sensitive people do better with higher karat gold, niobium or titanium.

Pros: A prestigious metal. Gold-fill is much better than gold-plating. The layer of gold in a gold-fill jump ring is approximately 100 times thicker than the gold in a plated layer, and it will not flake off as it does in plated jewelry.

Cons: Expensive!

Alloy: 14/20 Temper: Half Hard; Composition: Outer coating, approximately 58.5% gold, 13% silver, 24% copper, 4% zinc and 0.4 % cobalt; core, CDA 220 (90% copper, 10% zinc).

ANODIZED NIOBIUM

In its natural state, niobium is a dull gray. Niobium is colored by anodizing the rings (dipping them in an electrically charged solution). The colors obtained depend on the voltage. Colors may vary greatly from batch to batch.

Pros: Beautiful, vibrant colors. Hypoallergenic (though a select few still react to this metal, and are better off with titanium). Will not tarnish.

Cons: Expensive. Oils from skin may change the colors. Easily scratched, so be careful when weaving.

Alloy: pure niobium; Temper: Full Hard.

ANODIZED TITANIUM

Like niobium, titanium is colored by anodizing the rings and the colors obtained depend on the voltage. Colors usually vary within a batch, sometimes even within a single ring, and colors may vary greatly from batch to batch.

Pros: Very strong, yet lightweight. Hypoallergenic.

Cons: Expensive. Many of the colors are subtle, not as deep or vibrant as niobium and aluminum colors. Titanium work hardens easily, so do not bend your rings too far or too much, or they will break.

Alloy: TI-AL6-V4; Temper: One Quarter Hard; Composition: 90% titanium, 6% aluminum, 4% vanadium.

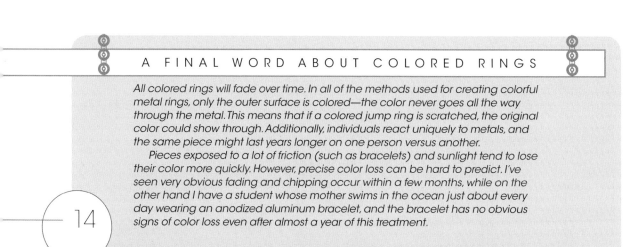

A FINAL WORD ABOUT COLORED RINGS

All colored rings will fade over time. In all of the methods used for creating colorful metal rings, only the outer surface is colored—the color never goes all the way through the metal. This means that if a colored jump ring is scratched, the original color could show through. Additionally, individuals react uniquely to metals, and the same piece might last years longer on one person versus another.

Pieces exposed to a lot of friction (such as bracelets) and sunlight tend to lose their color more quickly. However, precise color loss can be hard to predict. I've seen very obvious fading and chipping occur within a few months, while on the other hand I have a student whose mother swims in the ocean just about every day wearing an anodized aluminum bracelet, and the bracelet has no obvious signs of color loss even after almost a year of this treatment.

Ring Measurements

You may notice that I use many different jump ring sizes in this book. Sure, I have a few favorite sizes that are versatile enough to be used in multiple projects. However, there is no single size that can be used for all projects. Sometimes the ideal weave structure requires a ring that is ever-so-slightly larger or thicker than the ring I originally grabbed. I keep many ring sizes on hand—more than fifty sizes, to be precise—so that I never have to settle for a less-than-perfect fit.

Obviously, the chain mail hobbyist does not need to keep so many sizes. As much as possible, I've tried to use certain ring sizes over and over again so that you can tackle different projects with the same batches of rings. Some weaves are forgiving and will allow you to use a slightly different size without compromising the overall pattern. Others, however, are extremely precise and will not work if a single ring size is wrong. The more you weave, the more you'll develop a sense of which weaves are flexible in regard to ring sizes. I recommend that beginners use the ring sizes suggested for each project, but advanced chain mail weavers can feel free to try modifications right away.

When purchasing jump rings, it is important to know how they are measured, as there are many different methods. Some suppliers measure the inner diameter of the ring, and others use the outer diameter (typically bead suppliers who are accustomed to measuring the outer diameter of beads). Some prefer inches, some metric, and others alternate between both. Adding to the confusion, wire gauges are not consistent across metal types. You should always ask your supplier for the exact measurements of the rings to ensure you are buying what you need.

The jump rings in this book will be listed using a letter/number system. The letter represents the inner diameter of the ring and the number indicates the wire gauge. Conversions to traditional fractional inches and millimeters will be given, or you can use the charts in this section and on pages 140–141.

Anatomy of a jump ring

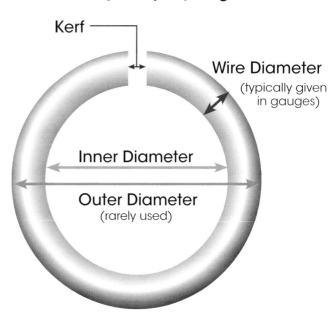

Kerf

Wire Diameter
(typically given in gauges)

Inner Diameter

Outer Diameter
(rarely used)

Hate math? Do charts full of numbers make your head spin? No worries. Because full conversions are listed for each ring size used in this book, you don't have to worry about the charts ahead, and can skip to Tools on page 18 if you choose. The following information is provided because I know a good number of people are interested. Chain mail is a hobby that attracts—or perhaps leads to!—persnickety attitudes toward ring sizing. I couldn't write a book and not include this information.

A typical ring listing looks like this:
H18—18 gauge, 3/16" (4.8mm)

In this example, H is the inner diameter of the mandrel the wire was coiled around. H represents 3/16" which converts to 4.8mm. The next piece of information (here, 18) is the gauge—you'll need to know if the metal is considered a base metal or precious metal in order to know the exact measurement indicated by the simple listing of "18."

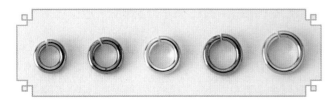

INNER DIAMETER

I use a letter to represent the inner diameter of my jump rings for a few reasons. First, it is far less cumbersome when teaching to say "H" rather than "three-sixteenths of an inch, also known as four point eight millimeters." Second, the mandrels used to make my jump rings increase in increments of 1/64 of an inch. Many people find it easier to understand that a sequence of increasing inner diameters is F, G, H rather than 5/32", 11/64", 3/16".

I use fractional inch mandrels for my rings because when I began making chain mail many years ago, that was the standard system used in the U.S. for chain mail armor, and all the suppliers I could find used those mandrels.

A year later, I adopted the lettering system from Spider, a chain mail artist from the San Francisco Bay area. Spider has a newer numbering system now, but I thought her lettering technique was ingenious, so I began using it in classes.

To understand exactly what the letters mean, refer to the chart at right. As you can see from the included measurements, letter D rings are smaller than E, which are smaller than F, and so on. Note that the letters refer to the size of the mandrel that the raw wire was wrapped around.

The chart shown here only shows a few of the options you have in rings. The full chart can be found on page 140.

The actual size of the inner diameter of the jump ring is usually slightly larger than the size of the mandrel. When raw wire is wrapped around a mandrel, it "relaxes" a bit after being coiled, because it is the nature of the wire to maintain its straight shape. This relaxing is known as springback.

Because different metals and tempers have such varied springback, standardizing ring sizes can be difficult. For example, a stainless steel jump ring wrapped around a P-size mandrel is significantly larger than a copper jump ring wrapped around the same mandrel. Steel is tougher, so it springs back more. In order to keep things simple, I like my rings to be the same size, no matter what metal. Therefore, all the rings I use have been standardized around Full Hard aluminum springback tolerances. For my rings, steel is coiled around mandrels that are ever-so-slightly smaller (sometimes as little as 1/128" or even 0.1mm, sometimes much more) and copper is coiled around slightly larger mandrels. The result is that I can usually mix and match amongst the base metals, rarely having to re-do the pattern to account for springback. If you are making your own rings you'll need to account for springback. If you purchase pre-made rings, the rings of some suppliers may work as is, and for others, you might have to make adjustments to the sizes.

Letter	Mandrel	aka	Decimal	Millimeter
D	8/64"	1/8"	0.125"	3.175
E	9/64"		0.141"	3.572
F	10/64"	5/32"	0.156"	3.969
G	11/64"		0.172"	4.366
H	12/64"	3/16"	0.188"	4.763

Chart Key

Letter = my shorthand abbreviation for the mandrel size
Mandrel = the size of the mandrel
aka = the reduced fractions typically used in the chain mail world; for example one would say 3/16" rather than 12/64"
Decimal = the inch measurement expressed as a decimal rather than a fraction. Listed here for math geeks, as well as those looking to calculate aspect ratios.
Millimeter = the millimeter equivalent of the mandrel size for the vast majority of the rest of the world, which uses the metric system

Jump rings created using a variety of wire gauges

Jump rings of different sizes, with the same aspect ratio

WIRE GAUGES

Gauge is a measure of the thickness of wire. Different numbering systems are used depending on the type of metal. Overall, as the gauge number decreases, the thickness of the wire increases. In other words, in the same metal, 24 gauge is always thinner than 22 gauge, which in turn, is thinner than 20 gauge. Because gauge systems can be somewhat arbitrary, many serious chain mail artists prefer to use wire measurements instead of gauge so that others know exactly what the wire size is.

The table below shows the wire diameter of the rings used in this book. Precious metals use the American Wire Gauge System (AWG), sometimes called Brown & Sharpe. Base metals generally use Standard Wire Gauge (SWG), with the exception of 20 gauge and 22 gauge base metal rings, which are also AWG. SWG is sometimes called Imperial Wire Gauge or British Standard Gauge.

Wire Gauge	Precious Metals*	Base Metals**
22	0.025" (0.6mm)	0.025" (0.6mm)
21	0.028" (0.72mm)	
20	0.032" (0.8mm)	0.032" (0.8mm)
19	0.036" (0.91mm)	
18	0.04" (1.02mm)	0.048" (1.22mm)
17	0.045" (1.15mm)	
16	0.051" (1.29mm)	0.062" (1.6mm)
15	0.057" (1.45mm)	
14	0.064" (1.63mm)	0.08" (2.05mm)
12	0.08" (2.05mm)	0.104" (2.64mm)
10	0.1" (2.59mm)	0.128" (3.25mm)

*Precious Metals include gold-fill, niobium, sterling silver and titanium (niobium gauges tend to deviate slightly from the typical AWG diameters)
**Base Metals include aluminum (including anodized aluminum), bronze, copper, jewelry brass and stainless steel

ASPECT RATIO

If the thought of math makes you cringe, feel free to skip this section—it isn't essential for making the pieces in this book. I've included it to sate those chain mail purists (myself among them) who feel that no chain mail book is complete without at least mentioning aspect ratio.

In chain mail, aspect ratio is a number that represents the relationship between the wire gauge and the inner diameter of a particular size jump ring. The exact formula to calculate aspect ratio is:

> inner diameter divided by wire diameter equals aspect ratio;

or, in shorthand:

> $ID \div WD = AR$

Note that the formula is wire diameter and not wire gauge. This is because, as we just discussed, different metals use different gauges, so "16 gauge" is not as precise as "1.6mm wire diameter." You must convert the gauge to either millimeters or inches (to match the measurement system used for the ring's ID).

If you have rings on hand, measure the diameters with calipers for maxium accuracy. Using calipers to measure inner diameter means springback is also measured, making your AR calculations as precise as possible.

I won't go into great technical detail about aspect ratio here, but if you're a serious chain mailer, you will want to find out more and understand aspect ratio. It makes choosing rings much easier. Instead of blindly trying different ring sizes, you can mathematically calculate which rings should work best for the weave. If you've made the Box weave on page 70 with an 18 gauge sterling silver ring, and you love how it looks, but want to make a 16 gauge version, you won't have to guess what size works. You'll simply calculate what 16 gauge ring has the same aspect ratio, and you'll use that. It's like putting a ring on a copier and hitting reduce or enlarge—the proportions remain the same, just the overall size increases or decreases.

A full aspect ratio chart is included on page 141, and if you'd like to learn even more about aspect ratio, check out the articles listed on page 141 as well.

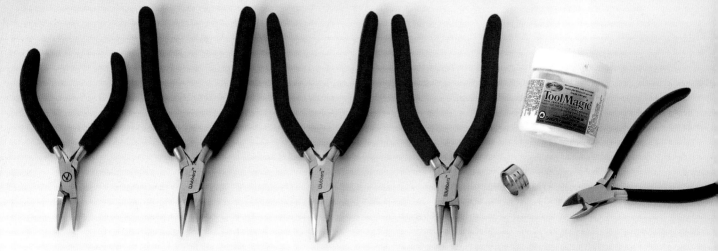

From left to right: flat-nose pliers, chain-nose pliers, bent-nose pliers, round-nose pliers, Tool Magic, jump ring tool, wire cutters

Tools

Pliers are the essential tool for chain mail weavers. They come in a variety of shapes and sizes, and there is no "One Tool Fits All." Everyone's hands are different; weavers should choose pliers based on palm size, finger length and hand strength. Additionally, different metals and ring sizes have different requirements, so if you use a mixture of metals and sizes, you'll likely wind up with several different pairs of pliers.

Plier jaws come in several shapes—those most commonly used for jewelry are flat-, chain-, bent- and round-nose. Round-nose pliers are used to make loops, and should not be used to manipulate jump rings. For chain mail, I prefer flat-nose pliers because I find they give me the best leverage. Occasionally, if I need to sneak into a tight spot, I'll use chain- or bent-nose pliers. Use whatever tool is most comfortable for you. Most bead shops sell a variety of pliers, and many will allow you to test them for fit and comfort. My personal favorites are:

—⊖ Lindstrom Rx pliers for small detail work, particularly 20 gauge rings and smaller in all metals. When the instructions in this book call for narrow flat-nose or thin-jawed pliers, these are an excellent choice, as the jaw is small enough to squeeze into tight spots.

—⊖ Euro Tool pliers for all-around work, mostly 18 gauge and 16 gauge in all metals except stainless steel and bronze.

—⊖ Wubbers wide, flat-nose pliers for stainless steel and bronze rings in 18 gauge and 16 gauge, as well as some 14 gauge rings in softer metals.

—⊖ Duckbill pliers for thick rings, usually 10 gauge to 12 gauge sterling silver, and 12 gauge to 14 gauge base metal. I sometimes use them for high aspect ratio 16 gauge rings in all metals.

I often dip my plier jaws in plastic coating—the brand I prefer is Tool Magic. The coating allows me to work faster without worrying about marring the rings or scratching off the color. I dip the pliers once, let them dry for a few hours, then dip again. (Two thin coats seem to last longer than one thick one.) When the coating gets grubby, I simply pull it off and re-dip. Actually, I prefer to have an extra set of already-dipped pliers on hand, in case the coating wears down while I'm in the middle of a project. With an extra coated pair on hand, I don't have to stop; I simply grab the fresh pliers and keep going. I'll then re-coat one or both pliers before I head to bed, so I'm all set to go the next morning.

I'm a two-pliers gal myself, but many of my students like to use a jump ring tool for opening their rings. The tool acts as your second set of pliers as you open the ring. To see this tool in use, flip to page 26. The only other tool used in this book is a pair of wire cutters. You don't have to add beads to any of these projects, but for those who like the look of beads, you'll need to use cutters to trim wire pieces before adding the beads used in these designs.

In the instructions sometimes you might notice that I switch between plier types and even between coated and non-coated pliers while making a single piece. Feel free to do the same—sometimes it is easier to work with smaller rings when the pliers are uncoated. Some days your hands may be tired, and therefore you might need to use a different pair of pliers to work comfortably. Again, use what works best for you to get the job done!

Additions and Embellishments

Once you've created a chain mail piece, you may need to add a component, such as a clasp or earwire, to make it wearable. You can add embellishments, as well.

FINDINGS

I recommend these common components—some of which are called findings in the jewelry industry—for finishing your jewelry pieces.

Toggle clasps are my preferred method of finishing bracelets. Other types of clasps have triggers that will break over time, making this non-mechanical clasp one of the most secure. Toggles are composed of two pieces, a loop and a bar, and they are especially secure if the loop is small and the bar is long. Toggles come in a myriad of shapes and sizes. Depending on my design, sometimes I choose a large, fancy clasp, and other times I feel the weave calls for a plain, understated one. For more on using toggle clasps, see page 35.

Lobster claw clasps are used for many necklaces in this book. When you use a lobster claw, be sure to weave a large, obvious ring for the claw to attach to. For ease of use, I recommend only using lobster claws that are 15mm or larger, especially in men's jewelry.

Slide clasps (sometimes called tube clasps) are perfect for flat and wide weaves. These clasps are made of two tubes—one is slightly smaller than the other, so that it can slide inside the larger tube. These clasps hardly take up any space, creating a seamless look for cuff bracelets. Most slide clasps have between two and five connection points on each side, though some wider clasps have as many as nine connection points. You may need to be creative when connecting your weaving to your clasp. See Steps 15–17 on pages 66–67 for an example of a way to connect a slide clasp to a finished piece of jewelry.

Pendant bails can be added to the top of a piece of chain mail, allowing the piece to be added to a chain as a pendant. Depending on the orientation of the connection point of your bail, you might need to add an extra jump ring so that the pendant will lay flat. If you choose a narrow bail, you may need to remove the clasp from your chain in order to add the pendant bail, then re-attach the clasp.

Earwires are the portions of earrings that go through the ear. I strongly prefer the earwire style known as French hooks. I also recommend rubber ear backs to keep earrings from sliding out of your ears. As with pendant bails, pay attention to the orientation of the connection loop and adjust the end of your chain as needed to give your finished piece the look you desire.

Eyepins and headpins are used for attaching beads. I prefer ball headpins, rather than flat headpins, because I think they give a piece of jewelry a more polished look.

BEADS

Though I occasionally use semi-precious stones, most of my beaded pieces contain crystals, and my favorite is Swarovski crystal. What can I say? I like sparkle! The sizes and shapes most commonly used in this book are 4mm bicones, 6mm rounds, 8mm rounds and vertically drilled 9mm drops. I often use 2mm seamless sterling beads on either side of the round crystals, and sometimes on top of the drops, for an added touch of sophistication.

PRE-MADE CHAIN

You might be surprised to see this in a book about making your own chain. However, pre-made chain can be a real time-saver. If you sell jewelry, it can make some of your pieces more affordable. Combine chain mail patches with pre-made chain to create a necklace that comes together much faster than if you wove the chain by hand.

When you connect chain mail to pre-made chain, you may need to add a small ring to the end of the chain in order to allow another, larger jump ring to pass through and attach your weave.

Techniques

If you want to become a confident and proficient chain mail weaver, you should master the following techniques. Use the easier weaves in this book, such as the *Basic Coiled Choker* on page 122, to practice these techniques until they are second nature to you.

I recommend that complete novices start out with rings in an inexpensive and pliable metal, such as aluminum or copper, that are 18 gauge and have an inner diameter of at least H (3/16" [4.8mm]). This size is large enough to easily see, but not so thick that it requires extra muscle power to manipulate.

CLOSING JUMP RINGS

If you're new to chain mail, it's a good idea to practice closing rings, as every ring needs to be closed at some point.

DO NOT DO THIS!

First off, let's discuss what not to do: Do not try to close the ring by sandwiching it with the pliers. It will only pop open again as soon as you let go.

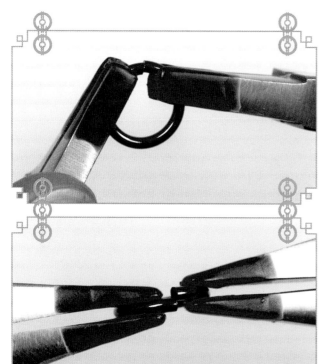

1 To begin, grip the ring with two pairs of pliers, one in each hand. Hold onto the ring near the kerf (the cut where the saw sliced through the metal). If you grip too far down on the ring, you won't have proper leverage. For more about proper grip, see Plier Grip on pages 22–23.

2 Here's another view of the ring gripped in the pliers. Notice how one side of the ring is already toward you (here, the left side).

3 Pull the far end toward you and push the near end away from you; at the same time, press the ends inward toward each other. This inward pressure is crucial, and without it, the ends of your ring will never fully meet when you let go of the pliers. Move the ends until their positions are reversed and the end that was originally farther away from you is now closer to you.

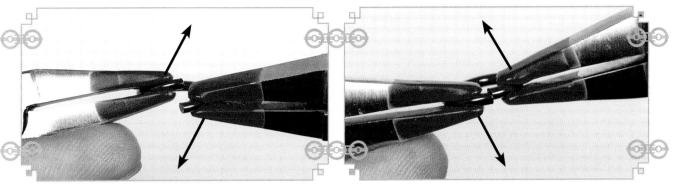

4 While you pull and push the ends (which I sometimes refer to as "wiggling"), the ends should overlap slightly as shown here, as this ultimately helps create a tightly closed ring.

5 Now that you've overlapped in one direction, begin to wiggle in the other direction, bringing the rings back into their original position. Overlapping in the other direction is crucial—if you only wiggle in one direction, your rings are likely to close improperly, or to not be perfectly flat.

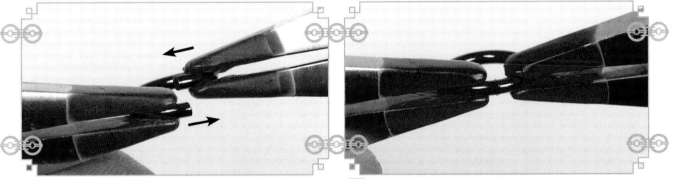

6 Again, as you wiggle, make sure to press the ends inward toward each other.

7 Once you've wiggled in both directions, bring the ends back to the center. During this step, many students are tempted to keep pushing inward, but it won't make a difference. You should only press inward during Steps 3–6 as you wiggle, not afterward. If you wait until the end, there's simply not enough space for the wire to move, so it won't maintain the "memory" of the inward pressure.

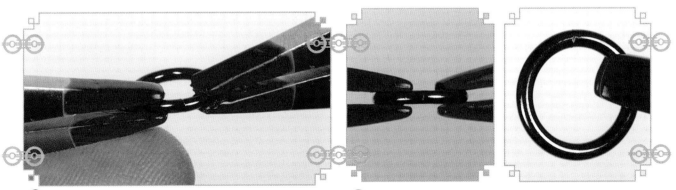

8 When you bring the ends flush, if they don't line up exactly—as shown above—make tiny wiggle adjustments until the jump ring closure is seamless.

9 Double check that the ring looks perfectly closed from the side as well as head-on.

QUICK WIGGLING

If you wiggle the ring too many times you may begin to compromise the strength of the metal, work-hardening it to the point of being brittle. Additionally, the more you wiggle the ring, the more likely you are to distort the circular shape.

Once you're comfortable with your pliers, aim to close the ring in three quick steps, taking approximately one to three seconds to complete all three steps. Notice how close the overlapped ends are—you shouldn't have to open the ring wide in order to close it.

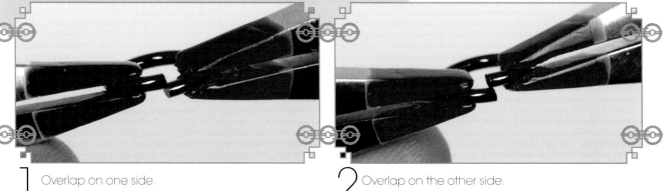

1 Overlap on one side.

2 Overlap on the other side.

3 Then close.

Tip

For most metals, you'll hear little clicks as the ends of the ring pass each other. That's a good sound! It means you're doing a good job of closing the kerf.

TIPS AND TRICKS FOR CLOSING RINGS

PLIER GRIP

Most people will not find it comfortable to grip both sides of the ring in the vertical position, or both sides in a horizontal position. I usually prefer to hold my pliers nearly at a right angle to one another, with the left pair of pliers almost straight up and down, and the right pair of pliers nearly horizontal. I'm still wiggling both ends of the ring, but I feel as though the vertical position of the left pliers gives me maximum leverage. However, your ideal grip is likely to be different from how I grip, simply because our bodies are different. I encourage you to experiment with different grips to see what works best for you.

A strict vertical grip makes it difficult to maneuver and puts extra stress on your joints.

You won't be able to get maximum leverage in a strict horizontal position, and it is tiring for your elbows.

This is an ideal grip for me; yours may be slightly different based on your hands and pliers.

For the best leverage, have your grip cover as much surface area as possible. When you hold the plier handles, your hands should be close to the jaws of the pliers, rather than lower (you may often see my thumbs right on the plier jaws); this will also increase your leverage.

Here, the grip is too low; if you hold your ring this way you will not have enough leverage.

In this example, the ring is gripped at an awkward angle. This is more likely to happen if you're using chain-nose pliers instead of flat-nose.

Covering the hole in the middle of the ring as shown above makes it hard to close the ring and hard to weave.

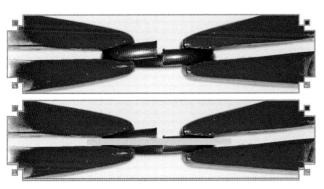

From an aerial view, the proper way to grip a jump ring is with the pliers—or more accurately, the space between the plier jaws—forming a straight line on either side of the ring as shown above.

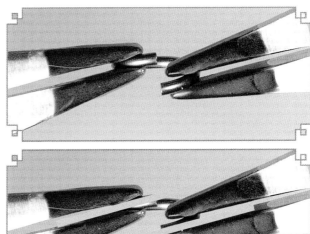

Maintain the proper grip even while wiggling. Even though your pliers no longer form a single straight line, they form two lines which remain parallel to each other.

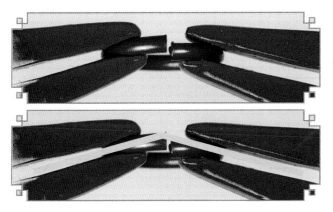

Beginners sometimes grip the rings at a bent angle as shown here. This may lead to marring the jump rings, as you don't have as much leverage as with the proper grip. Additionally, you are likely to create bent rings (see Saddle-Shaped Rings on page 24).

Tip

When manipulating jump rings, concentrate on initiating your movements from your shoulders, rather than your elbows or your wrists. By involving your entire arm, you will have more control and you will put less stress on your smaller, more injury-prone joints, especially the wrists. When working with tough metals, you'll need those bigger muscles to bend steel—literally! If you only work from your wrists or your elbows, you will quickly become sore and won't have the flexibility to maneuver new rings in and out of the weave.

OVERBITE

Sometimes you may close a ring and find it has an "overbite." This is particularly true of high aspect ratio rings (rings in which the inner diameter is quite large compared with the thickness of the wire). With experience, you'll adjust the way you open and close high AR rings to prevent overbites. However, if you do encounter the occasional overbite, correcting is easy.

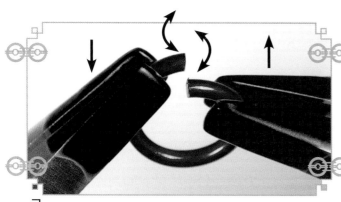

1 To adjust, wiggle the ring as normal (as shown by the middle arrows), but as you apply inward pressure, concentrate on pushing down on the side that needs to go down, and pulling up on the other side (as shown by the outer arrows).

2 You may need to do this a couple of times before the ends finally meet as they should.

SADDLE-SHAPED RINGS

Some beginners find that they are creating malformed saddle-shaped rings. This usually occurs if you are gripping the rings in the improper method shown on page 23.

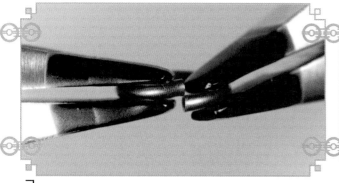

1 To correct, re-wiggle the ends past each other, and as you do so, overcompensate by fanning your pliers outward opposite of the curve of the saddle. It may help to open your elbows wide as you wiggle, so you maintain the proper angle.

2 A saddled ring may never be perfectly straight, but you should be able to make it significantly straighter by following this technique. If you can't, just start fresh with a new ring, being sure to grip in the proper position.

SEAMED CLOSURE

Your rings should be perfectly closed. Sometimes you may think a ring is closed, but if you hold it up to the light, you'll see a hairline gap at the kerf. Even though the line may seem insignificant to you, it may still be large enough to catch body hair and stray fuzzies from clothing. You'll need to wiggle the ends back and forth, being sure to push inward strongly when overlapping.

This is not a perfect closure because a hairline seam is visible.

TOO MUCH OVERLAPPING

If you're overlapping the rings so much that it is very difficult for you to pull the ends apart in order to overlap the other direction— congratulations, you are quite strong! You'll need to ease up on your pressure so that you can quickly overlap in one direction, and then the other (see Quick Wiggling on page 22).

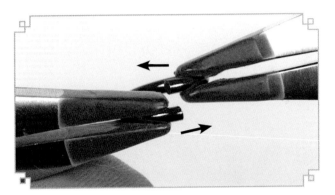

CLOSING TOUGH RINGS

Strong rings, such as those made from stainless steel and bronze, or any rings with low aspect ratios, can be difficult to close seamlessly. Remember that your first movement, even when opening a ring, is to bring the ends of the wire past each other as you are pushing inward (see Steps 3–4 in Closing Jump Rings on pages 20–21). If you do not push inward right away, the ring work hardens in an open position, and it will be even more difficult to bring the ends together later.

In the Quick Wiggling section on page 22, I mention that you shouldn't have to open the ring wide in order to close it. However, for tough metals, you might need to open the ring wider than normal—pushing inward as hard as you can as you open—in order to give enough space for the ends to overlap. I recommend adding a plastic coating to your plier jaws to avoid slipping while working with tough rings.

You don't have to open most rings very far in order to overlap the ends.

For tough rings, you might have to open wider to have leverage to push inward with sufficient pressure.

OPENING JUMP RINGS

If you understand how to close a jump ring, opening one is a breeze. Remember that every open jump ring eventually needs to be closed. Even though you are "opening" the ring, your first step in opening is an inward motion, just like closing.

It doesn't matter which direction the ring ends start out. I recommend that right-handers open the right side of the ring toward you. Left-handers, open the left side toward you. As you open, don't forget to press inward.

Right side of the ring open for right-handers

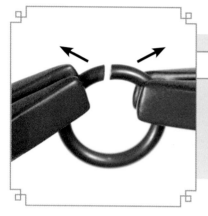

DO NOT DO THIS!

Do not try to open the ring by pulling the ends outward. Yes, the ring will open, but it will be difficult—if not impossible—to close it back into a perfect circle.

Left side of the ring open for left-handers

I prefer opening the right side toward me, because it positions the leading edge of the ring away from me. This means I can enter the weave from the front, rather than trying to blindly enter from the back.

Weaving from the front, with a ring opened according to your dominant hand, allows you to better see the path of the ring as you weave. You'll always hold the weave with your non-dominant hand.

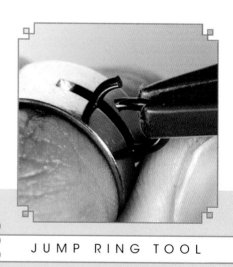

JUMP RING TOOL

I'm a two-pliers gal myself, but many of my students like to use a jump ring tool for opening their rings. Slip the ring on your non-dominant hand, grasp a raw (meaning straight from the bag) ring with your pliers, and slip it into the appropriate groove in the tool. Most tools have 2-4 openings of different widths. The tool acts as your second set of pliers as you open the ring.

You should open the rings just wide enough to be able to weave through (or scoop up) other rings of the needed gauge. If you don't open wide enough, you'll have difficulty getting your ring to go where it needs to go. If you open too wide, you'll likely have trouble closing your ring in a nice, neat circle, and you could also accidentally cross through rings that you're not supposed to go through.

This opening isn't wide enough to easily go through another ring of the same gauge.

This opening is too wide.

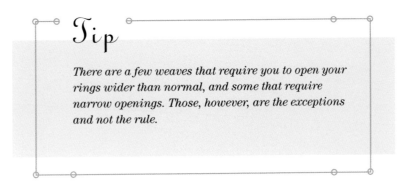

Tip

There are a few weaves that require you to open your rings wider than normal, and some that require narrow openings. Those, however, are the exceptions and not the rule.

This opening is just right for most weaves.

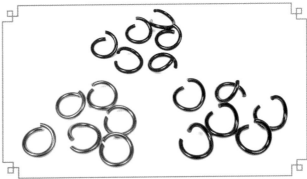

From top, clockwise: blue "just right" open rings; red rings open too far; orange rings open not far enough

After you open the ring and weave it through your weave, follow Steps 5–9 in Closing Jump Rings on page 21 to close your ring. You only need to overlap in one direction now, because you already overlapped in the other direction when you opened the ring.

WEAVING JUMP RINGS

Now that you know how to properly open and close jump rings, here are some techniques that are crucial to weaving quickly, smoothly and comfortably.

LEARN TO SCOOP

Many weaves call for you to add closed or raw jump rings to an open ring. It is best to use your pliers to pick up and weave these rings—fingers tend to be too large and clumsy. Sure, it may initially feel awkward when using pliers, but you'll likely find yourself adapting more quickly than you think to your new "fingers."

1 When you grasp an open ring with your pliers, try to grab it in the 2 o'clock/3 o'clock position if you're right-handed, or in the 9 o'clock/10 o'clock position if you're left-handed.

2 Use a soft surface such as a bead mat or a piece of fleece so you can press down slightly into the surface with the open jump ring to get under the other rings.

3 Bring the leading edge of the scooping ring up through the center of the rings.

4 Voila! You're ready to weave these added rings.

KEEP THE PLIERS AND THE WEAVE IN YOUR HAND

Learn this trick as soon as you can, because if you get in the habit of setting your pliers on the table as you weave, it will be a tough habit to break! As you add new rings, not only do you want to keep the weave in your hands, but you also want to keep your pliers in your hands at all times. If you need to use your fingers for something, move the pliers back in your hands so your fingers are free.

Pliers moved to the back of my hand, while the front holds the weave

HOLD THE WEAVE TIGHTLY

In the example below, I need to weave an open ring through 6 closed rings that are already part of the weave. I'm holding the 6 rings taut with my non-dominant hand. This means they won't slip and slide around as I add the new ring. You should always hold as tightly as possible without covering up the path for the new ring.

Note that you won't always see me doing this in the step-by-step photos. For clarity, I want you to see enough of the weave to understand where to add new rings. If all you saw were my thumbs, that would make this book very boring and difficult to understand indeed!

DON'T BE AFRAID TO DO THE CHICKEN DANCE!

You should never feel like a contortionist as you weave. I've seen students in extremely awkward positions as they try to get a ring through their weave. The problem: They're trying to do all the movements from their wrist, rather than their elbows and shoulders.

To solve this, know that you often need to open your elbows wide as you enter the weave. When you bring your elbows back toward your sides, the ring glides through like magic. Yes, you might look a little like a chicken, but it is far more comfortable—not to mention better for your joints—than trying to contain all the movement from the wrist down.

BASIC WIRE LOOP

This technique allows you to easily add beads and other embellishments to your chain mail. It's also the building block for other wire techniques. For this technique you'll need: a small piece of wire, a bead with a hole large enough to accommodate the wire, two pairs of flat-nose pliers and one pair each of round-nose pliers and wire cutters. You could also substitute a pre-fabricated eyepin or headpin for the piece of wire; if you do this, begin from Step 6.

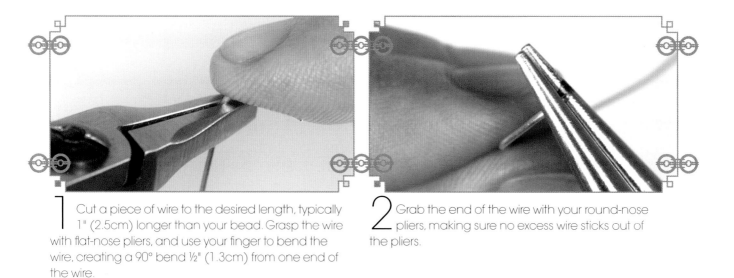

1 Cut a piece of wire to the desired length, typically 1" (2.5cm) longer than your bead. Grasp the wire with flat-nose pliers, and use your finger to bend the wire, creating a 90° bend ½" (1.3cm) from one end of the wire.

2 Grab the end of the wire with your round-nose pliers, making sure no excess wire sticks out of the pliers.

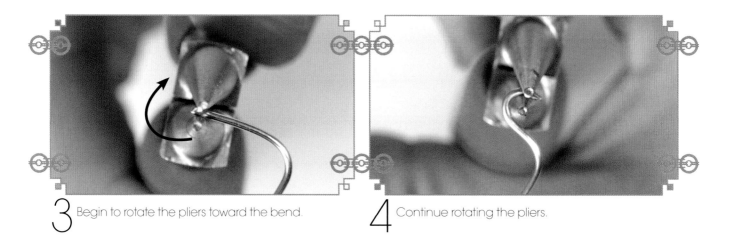

3 Begin to rotate the pliers toward the bend.

4 Continue rotating the pliers.

MAKING YOUR MARK

Use a permanent marker to draw a line on your plier jaws to indicate where to position your wire based on how big you want your loop to be. (This is especially helpful when you are trying to match the size of a pre-made eyepin. Slide the eyepin onto your round-nose pliers and you'll know exactly where to wrap the wire to duplicate the loop size precisely.) The closer you work to the tip of the pliers, the smaller the loop will be (and the less wire you'll need). For larger loops, use more wire and position it on the jaw closer to the handles of the pliers. If you always create your loops following your marker line, each loop will be exactly the same size!

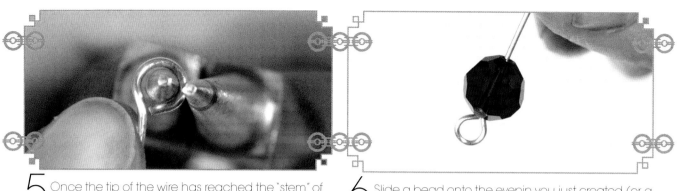

5 Once the tip of the wire has reached the "stem" of the wire, one loop has been created (this is what a pre-made eyepin looks like).

6 Slide a bead onto the eyepin you just created (or a pre-made eyepin or headpin, if that is your choice).

You can treat the loop like a jump ring and wiggle the end of the wire closed if it isn't quite touching. Use the same "jump ring" idea to open the loop and attach it to another loop or to a jump ring or another component. Never try to "unroll" and re-roll a loop, as the wire will not stay smooth.

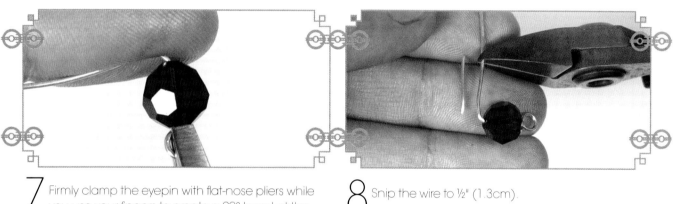

7 Firmly clamp the eyepin with flat-nose pliers while you use your fingers to create a 90° bend at the free end of the wire.

8 Snip the wire to ½" (1.3cm).

9 Repeat Steps 2–5 to complete a second loop.

10 Using two pairs of flat-nose pliers, grasp the loops and wiggle them gently until each loop emerges in the same straight line from the bead.

When you create your second loop it should face the opposite direction of the first loop. This helps create a more symmetrical wire shape.

31

WIRE WRAP

After you're fluent in basic loops, try wire wrapping. Wire wraps are more secure than basic loops because they are permanently closed; however, because of this you cannot open and close them like you can basic loops. Jump rings are used to connect wire wraps to your chain mail.

To make a wire wrap, you'll need: a small piece of wire, a bead with a hole large enough to accommodate the wire, and one pair each of round-nose pliers, flat-nose pliers, bent-nose pliers, chain-nose pliers and wire cutters. For this demonstration, 8mm crystals and a generous 2½" (6.4cm) length of wire were used. If you only need wire wrapping on one side of the bead, substitute a pre-made headpin for the piece of wire and begin from Step 11.

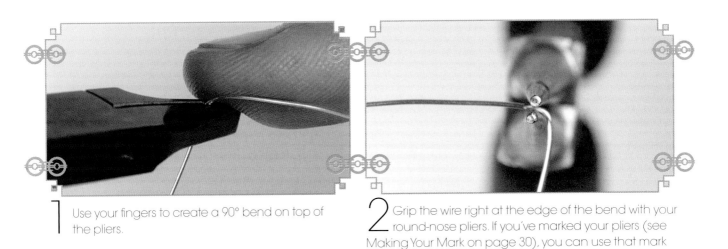

1 Use your fingers to create a 90° bend on top of the pliers.

2 Grip the wire right at the edge of the bend with your round-nose pliers. If you've marked your pliers (see Making Your Mark on page 30), you can use that mark here to create loops of the same size.

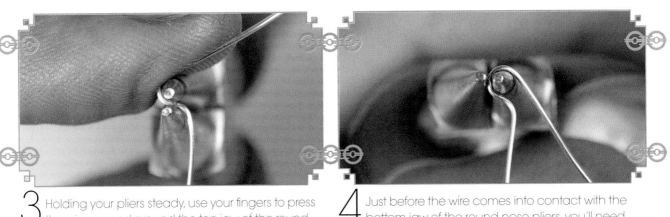

3 Holding your pliers steady, use your fingers to press the wire up and around the top jaw of the round-nose pliers.

4 Just before the wire comes into contact with the bottom jaw of the round-nose pliers, you'll need to adjust your plier position. Open the jaws of the pliers slightly and rotate the pliers inside the wire so that the bottom jaw is on the left. (Note that in the previous photo the pliers were vertical, and now they are horizontal.)

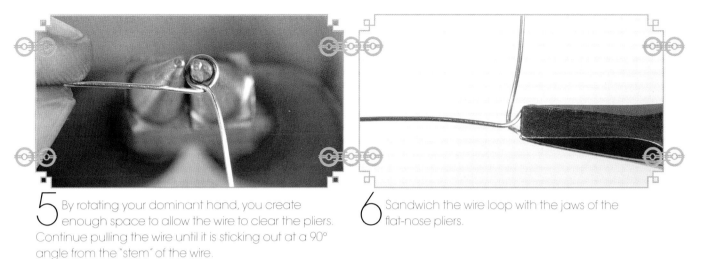

5 By rotating your dominant hand, you create enough space to allow the wire to clear the pliers. Continue pulling the wire until it is sticking out at a 90° angle from the "stem" of the wire.

6 Sandwich the wire loop with the jaws of the flat-nose pliers.

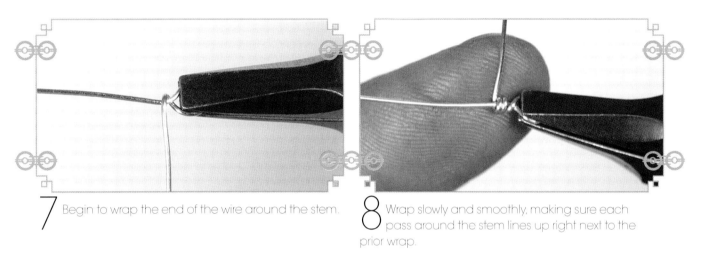

7 Begin to wrap the end of the wire around the stem.

8 Wrap slowly and smoothly, making sure each pass around the stem lines up right next to the prior wrap.

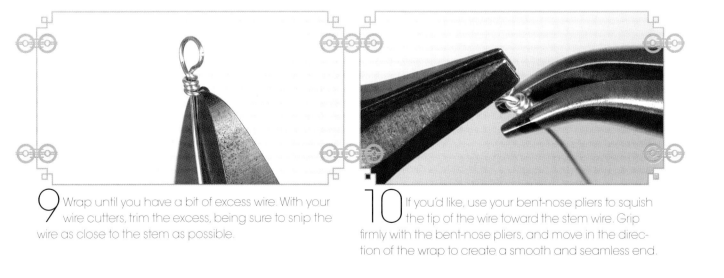

9 Wrap until you have a bit of excess wire. With your wire cutters, trim the excess, being sure to snip the wire as close to the stem as possible.

10 If you'd like, use your bent-nose pliers to squish the tip of the wire toward the stem wire. Grip firmly with the bent-nose pliers, and move in the direction of the wrap to create a smooth and seamless end.

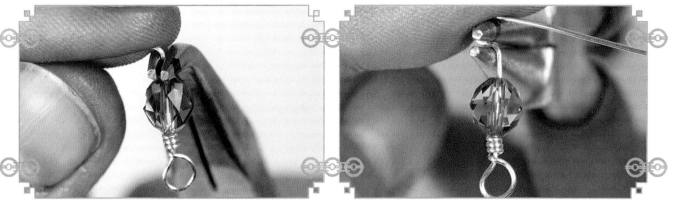

11 Add your bead onto the wire, and create another 90° bend on top of the bead. To allow space for the wrap, grip the wire with chain- or bent-nose pliers just above the bead, and create your bend on the pliers.

Make sure the bend is oriented so that your second loop will be on the same plane as the first loop, not perpendicular to it.

12 Pull the wire up and over the round-nose pliers as in Steps 2–4 to create a second loop.

Tip

Eventually you should mark your chain- or bent-nose pliers with a permanent marker in the exact spot that you need to grip in Step 11, based on how many wraps you prefer. Too much space, and you'll have a long "stem" requiring many wraps to cover. Too little space, and you'll only be able to go around once. I find the most elegant wraps have 3–4 rotations on each end.

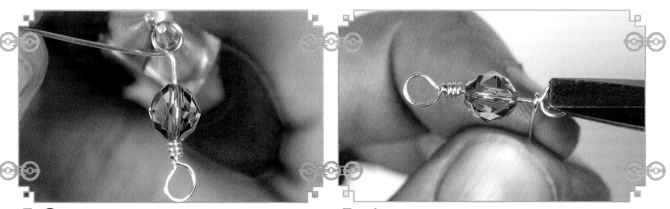

13 As in Step 5, continue pulling the wire end until you have a new 90° angle.

14 Repeat Steps 6–10 to finish the wrap on the second side.

Finishing Touches

Most projects in this book contain detailed instructions for bringing your piece to an elegant finish. However, these quick tips can be used on any project.

Make a mini chain of jump rings to provide enough slack to easily connect and disconnect a toggle clasp. The chain should be the exact length of the bar portion of the toggle when it is turned.

I make most of my women's necklaces adjustable, especially ones that might be worn over a sweater in the winter. I do this by creating a simple chain of jump rings on one end. To make it prettier, you can also add a bead or colored jump rings to the end.

Care and Feeding of Your Mail

Follow these tips to give your chain mail jewelry a long and healthy life!

— Always handle your jewelry gently. Remember that most chain mail links are not soldered closed, and can therefore be pulled open. Treat your chain mail just as you would handle a delicate pearl necklace or crystal bracelet.

— When not wearing your jewelry, store each piece in its own bag and keep the bag in a dark place. This reduces tarnish, keeps softer metals from being scratched and preserves colored rings longer. You can use a soft fabric bag or, to prevent tarnish, a sealed zip-top plastic bag. To further help prevent tarnish, add an anti-tarnish tab to the bag.

— To clean enameled copper, along with gold- and silver-colored metals such as sterling silver, stainless steel, aluminum (including anodized aluminum), titanium, niobium and gold-fill, soak jewelry in water with non-lotion dishwashing soap for several minutes. Then, lather with a new drop of soap and gently but briskly rub the jewelry between your palms. Rinse with warm water and let the jewelry air-dry, or use a blow dryer on its lowest and coolest setting.

— To clean tarnish from "red" metals including copper, bronze and brass, soak your pieces in a mixture of pure lemon juice and salt for five to thirty seconds. (You may use this method even if your jewelry also contains anodized aluminum or enameled copper rings.) After removing the jewelry from the mixture, lather with non-lotion dishwashing soap and water, and rub the jewelry gently but briskly between your palms. Rinse it thoroughly, then pat it dry with a towel or use a blow dryer on its lowest setting. Make sure the piece is fully dry before you return it to its resealable bag.

— For a spectacular shine, most chain mail can be polished in a rock tumbler. Small rotary tumblers are readily available at rock shops and online. Add stainless steel shot (small BBs) and burnishing compound to water before tumbling—the shot acts as thousands of tiny hammers to pound out slight imperfections in the rings. If you are not using shot, make sure to tumble several pieces at once so that there is enough friction to shine the rings. Care should be taken when tumbling pieces with beads, as crystals could shatter and some semi-precious stones should not be soaked in water.

— Keep jewelry away from household cleaners and chlorine, unless you're eager to experiment with at-home patinas. Avoid wearing your jewelry during periods of exertion, as sweat can corrode jewelry.

— Avoid resting sterling silver directly on wood surfaces, especially oak, as wood finishes usually contain acids that can mar the surface of sterling. Always store silver away from direct sunlight.

How to Use this Book
DIFFICULTY AND TIME RATINGS

I designed this book to appeal to both beginning and advanced students. The projects are divided into four chapters, each with a focus on a particular core weave or technique: Japanese, Byzantine, Helm and Coiled. Within each chapter, the projects generally progress in order of difficulty. Each project has a rating from one to four rings:

1 ring = Beginner
Little to no prior knowledge required.

2 rings = Intermediate
Knowledge of the core weave or technique for that chapter required.
Some knowledge of techniques from previous chapters may be required.

3 rings = Advanced
Fluency with the core weave is required. Knowledge of techniques from previous chapters is likely to be needed. Ability to work with tiny rings or stiff rings may be required.

4 rings = Expert
Highly intricate or difficult-to-execute designs requiring meticulous technique and complete comfort with prior weaves in that chapter. Knowledge of techniques from previous chapters is likely to be needed.

The first few projects in each chapter are very detailed; each step is clearly laid out. In the first chapter, many basic techniques are reiterated in the introductory projects to make sure beginners have adequate time to become comfortable working with jump rings. Later projects in each chapter are laid out with the assumption that you have prior knowledge and will gloss over certain steps and techniques. Flip back to previous chapters for a refresher anytime you need to.

New chain mailers can choose to complete the first one or two projects in each chapter, and then return to tackle advanced and expert weaves later. Some students may prefer to focus on a particular chapter and progress through beginning, intermediate and advanced projects, developing a full understanding of the chapter technique before moving on to other chapters.

To help you gauge how long a piece will take, each project has a "time" rating from Quick to Epic.

For your convenience, I've provided estimated times go along with each rating, but I want to emphasize that each person weaves at a very different weaving speed, so these are very rough estimates. Additionally, the rating is based on the average student working on the project for the second or third time through. You will need more time if you are creating the project for the first time.

Quick—Under 1 hour
Instant gratification!

Long—4–7 hours
You may need up to a full day to complete this project, and will definitely need to take breaks.

Mid-length—1–4 hours
You can complete the project in one sitting, but you'll probably need breaks.

Epic—7+ hours
You are unlikely to complete this project in one day.

SUPPLIES

Each project has a complete list of needed supplies. The jump ring sizes are listed in shorthand code, as well as converted to fractional inches and millimeters. Refer to the wire gauge chart on page 17 to determine the exact wire diameters of the rings. Precious metals used in this book are always AWG; base metals, including copper, are SWG for 19 gauge and thicker, AWG for 20 gauge and thinner. Remember, though: Jump ring sizing is unfortunately not universal, and different suppliers' ring sizes may or may not work.

Because the rings I use have been standardized, within a metal group (AWG or SWG) you can mix and match. For instance, if a weave lists copper rings, but you prefer aluminum rings, you can almost always substitute aluminum rings of the same size because they are both base metals. If, however, you wish to create a gold-fill piece, you'll need to refer to the size conversions for that project. Conversions are usually approximate—I have tested them with my rings, but the piece is likely to behave slightly differently from the original project. Sizes will always be listed in the same order as in the original materials list; clasp ring sizes are often omitted. Alternate sizes are occasionally listed, should you wish to create a heftier or more delicate piece. Again, however, note that you may need to adjust the size ring needed based on how your supplier creates and measures rings.

The final length is listed for bracelets and necklaces. The average women's bracelet size is between 7"–7½" (17.8cm–19.0cm); the average men's size is between 8"–8½" (20.3cm–21.6cm). Women's necklaces range in average length from 16" (40.6cm) for a choker to 18"–20" (45.7cm–50.8cm) for a standard length necklace, and 24"–30" (61.0cm–76.2cm) for a long neck chain. Nearly all of the projects adhere to these standards. You may need to size your piece smaller or larger, and therefore will use fewer or more supplies than are listed.

Any tools you'll need are listed directly under the supplies. Refer to Tools on page 18 for a listing of the different kinds of pliers you can choose. Plastic coating such as Tool Magic is never listed as a requirement, but if you are scratching the rings or having difficulty gripping the rings with your pliers, I recommend dipping the jaws in a plastic coating.

INSTRUCTIONS

Before attempting any project, skim the entire set of instructions first, so that you will have a big-picture idea of what you'll be doing. If you're a veteran weaver or if you have highly developed visual spatial abilities, you might realize there's an alternate way to weave that works better for you, or you might be able to skip a few steps here and there.

Preparation for most weaves consists of opening and closing rings so that once you begin weaving, you can concentrate on learning the pattern, rather than worrying about opening and closing rings as you go. However, this is not a requirement. If you're comfortable diving right in, then please do so.

Most repetitive weaves provide a "weave in a nutshell" overview. Advanced chain mailers may be able to figure out the entire weave simply by studying the weave in a nutshell. For other chain mailers, the weave in a nutshell serves as an easy way to remember the basic steps of the weave. Once you're comfortable with the weave, you won't need to use the step by steps; you'll simply be able to look at the weave in a nutshell as a reminder of what to do next.

A WORD TO LEFTIES

Anyone who has taken classes with me knows that I am adamant about creating left-handed instructions. Do not think I've abandoned you, but—alas!—it is not feasible to create a second book with reversed photographs aimed at left-handed students. If you're having difficulty understanding a weave because of its handed-ness, I recommend propping a mirror in front of the book so you can see the photos from a left-hand perspective. Whenever the text mentions "right" or "left" you should reverse those directions. And don't forget to open the left side of the ring toward you (see page 26)!

Japanese

Our journey begins with the Japanese family of weaves. We start here because the basic pattern is one of the simplest to comprehend. The weaves in this family are characterized by horizontal rings that link vertical rings. Many beginning students intuit that all chain mail weaves are "horizontal linking to vertical," but as you'll see in later chapters, rings can be linked at a variety of angles. This chapter focuses mainly on variations of the Japanese 12-in-2 weave (shown in the *Reversible Japanese Lace Bracelet* on page 52), which is a fully doubled version of the ancient 6-in-1 pattern known as *asa no ha gusari* (gusari is Japanese for "chain").

If you are new to chain mail, I suggest that you start at the beginning of this chapter with the *Easy Earrings* pattern on page 40. As you begin, concentrate on getting accustomed to working with jump rings and developing your technique, then continue that process as you create the first few pieces in this chapter.

If you already have chain mail experience, you can hone your skills on more intricate patterns such as the lace-like *Japanese Diamond Bracelet* on page 62. Throughout the chapter, challenge yourself to try different color palettes or link smaller units together, as I did with the *Japanese Cross Bracelet* on page 47.

The horizontal-vertical connections in Japanese patterns are a great starting point for inventing new motifs and variations, as the weaves are easily expanded in the left/right direction as well as diagonally. The rings practically shout to be rearranged, resized and regrouped to form new designs. It is no coincidence that I have invented more weaves in the Japanese family than in any other family.

I encourage you to play with the Japanese weaves. Note the symmetry and order that dominates the patterns, and tweak these elements. Change ring sizes, use different colors to bring out various geometric shapes or add beads for an elegant finish. In short—set yourself free to explore the depths of these readily adaptable patterns.

A word of warning, though—don't expect the advanced pieces to come together quickly. With their plethora of tiny rings, these designs can be real time-eaters. As far as I'm concerned, the more meticulous the weave, the better, but I've also been called a glutton for punishment....

Easy Earrings

 *beginner*

MATERIALS LIST

6 large jump rings: P16 anodized aluminum, color gold—16 gauge, 5/16" (7.9mm)

8 small jump rings: F18 anodized aluminum, color purple—18 gauge, 5/32" (4.0mm)

2 earwires

TOOLS

2 pairs of flat-nose pliers

PRECIOUS METAL RING SUBSTITUTIONS

Large rings: O14—14 gauge, 19/64" (7.5mm)

Small rings: F18—18 gauge, 5/32" (4.0mm)

These earrings come together quickly, making them a perfect project for beginners. However, the color and sizing variations are endless—as you'll see on the next few pages—so more advanced students can feel free to experiment right off the bat. This pattern is great piece to have in your repertoire should you need to whip up a pair of earrings before you head out for a night on the town.

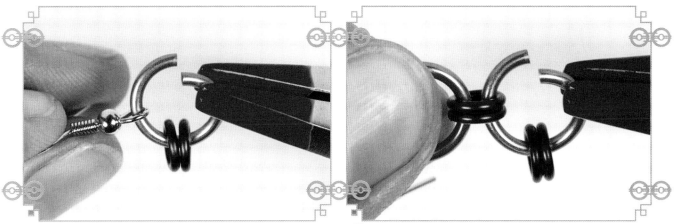

1 To prepare, close the small rings and open the large rings (see Closing Jump Rings on pages 20–25 and Opening Jump Rings on pages 26–27).
Scoop 2 small rings onto an open large ring (see Learn to Scoop on page 28). Before closing, add an earwire to the large ring.

2 With a new large ring, scoop up 2 new small rings, then weave the large ring through the 2 small rings from Step 1. It helps to pinch the previous small rings between your thumb and index finger for stability. Close the large ring.

3 With another large ring, go through the 2 small rings added in Step 2. Close the large ring, and you're done! Repeat Steps 1–3 for a second earring.

Tip

If your earwire loop is perpendicular to the hook instead of parallel to it, add a very small ring to the loop first, and hook your chain mail onto that ring. Otherwise, your earring won't be facing forward.

Try these earrings in your favorite colors, or make a pair to match a favorite outfit.

Now that you've mastered some of the very basic techniques, have fun playing with color and testing out different size ring combinations. Here are some of my favorites, from fun, everyday earrings to elegant and sophisticated adornments. Ring sizes are listed starting with the ring closest to the earwire and ending with the bottom ring for a single earring. Double the total quantity of rings listed to make two earrings.

Note that 14 and 12 gauge rings can be difficult to work with. I recommend using duckbill pliers dipped in a protective coating to help prevent marring the rings. Also, some of these variations require you to double the large rings. You can get plenty of practice doubling rings while passing them through smaller hanging rings in the *Reversible Japanese Lace Bracelet* on pages 52–55.

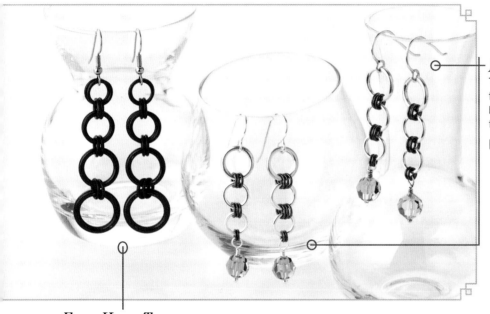

Niobium Crystals

This pattern also has tapering rings, but these go from large to small. A crystal bead at the end of the earring adds a touch of elegance.

PRECIOUS METAL, AWG

1 ring size O14—14 gauge, 19/64" (7.5mm)

3 rings size D20—20 gauge, 1/8" (3.2mm)

1 ring size N16—16 gauge, 9/32" (7.1mm)

3 rings size D20—20 gauge, 1/8" (3.2mm)

1 ring size J17—17 gauge, 7/32" (5.6mm)

2 rings size B20—20 gauge, 3/32" (2.4mm)

To add the crystal at the bottom, wire wrap an 8mm crystal bead on a 1¼" (3.2cm) headpin (see Wire Wrap on pages 32–34). Make the loop large enough to fit two 20 gauge rings.

Four-Hoop Taper

These striking earrings taper from smaller doubled rings to larger single rings. You can make yours in a single color like the ones shown here, or try a variety of colors.

BASE METAL, SWG

2 rings size L18—18 gauge, 1/4" (6.4mm)

2 rings size H18—18 gauge, 3/16" (4.8mm)

2 rings size P16—16 gauge, 5/16" (7.9mm)

2 rings size H18—18 gauge, 3/16" (4.8mm)

1 ring size T14—14 gauge, 3/8" (9.5mm)

2 rings size H18—18 gauge, 3/16" (4.8mm)

1 ring size X12—12 gauge, 7/16" (11.1mm)

Basic Crescent Earrings

This simple and versatile design uses rings of different sizes at the bottom to create a crescent shape.

BASE METAL, SWG

1 ring size H18—18 gauge, 3/16" (4.8mm)

2 rings size F18—18 gauge, 5/32" (4.0mm)

1 ring size L16—16 gauge, 1/4" (6.4mm)

2 rings size F18—18 gauge, 5/32" (4.0mm)

At the bottom: 1 ring size P16—16 gauge, 5/16" (7.9mm) stacked with 1 ring size H18—18 gauge 3/16" (4.8mm) on each side

Intricate Sterling Crescent Earrings

STERLING SILVER, AWG

1 ring size F17—17 gauge, 5/32" (4.0mm)

3 sets of B21 x 2—21 gauge, 3/32" (2.4mm)

2 sets of D19 x 2—19 gauge, 1/8" (3.2mm)

1 ring size H17—17 gauge, 3/16" (4.8mm)

3 sets of D19 x 2—19 gauge, 1/8" (3.2mm)

2 sets of E18 x 2—18 gauge, 9/64" (3.6mm)

At the bottom: 1 ring size O14—14 gauge, 19/64" (7.5mm) stacked with 1 ring size J17—17 gauge, 7/32" (5.6mm) on each side

To create a mini pair of Intricate Sterling Crescent Earrings, remove the H17 ring and the 3 sets of D19 rings just below it.

Beaded Bull's-Eye Earrings

Do you have leftover beads? Incorporate them into a quick pair of earrings to add a bit of flair.

BASE METAL, SWG

1 ring size F18—18 gauge, 5/32" (4.0mm)

2 rings size F18—18 gauge, 5/32" (4.0mm)

1 ring size R18—18 gauge, 11/32" (8.7mm)

2 rings size F18—18 gauge, 5/32" (4.0mm)

1 ring size R18—18 gauge, 11/32" (8.7mm)

2 rings size F18—18 gauge, 5/32" (4.0mm)

1 ring size R18—18 gauge, 11/32" (8.7mm)

Trapping the Beads

1 Trap a bead on a piece of wire following the Basic Wire Loop instructions on pages 30–31. Space your basic loops at the same distance as the sides of the jump ring. Slip one loop onto the jump ring, and use your fingers to slip on the other loop.

2 When you close the jump ring, the bead should be perfectly trapped in the center. If the length of your looped wire isn't long enough, the bead will rest to one side or another. That's an easy fix—simply re-do the loops, but make them larger this time.

Japanese Cross Earrings

 *beginner*

 *Quick project*

MATERIALS LIST

14 large jump rings: K16 copper—16 gauge, 15/64" (6.0mm)

20 small jump rings: F19 enameled copper—19 gauge, 5/32" (4.0mm)

16 color seafoam

4 color gunmetal

2 earwires

TOOLS

2 pairs of flat-nose pliers

small piece of wire (optional)

PRECIOUS METAL RING SUBSTITUTIONS

Large rings: J14—14 gauge, 7/32" (5.6mm)

Small rings: F18—18 gauge, 5/32" (4.0mm)

This pattern was one of the first earring designs I created, and it quickly became one of my most popular designs. Once you learn the basic pattern, have fun by varying the colors, linking additional components or adding beads. As you'll see on the next few pages, the possibilities are endless!

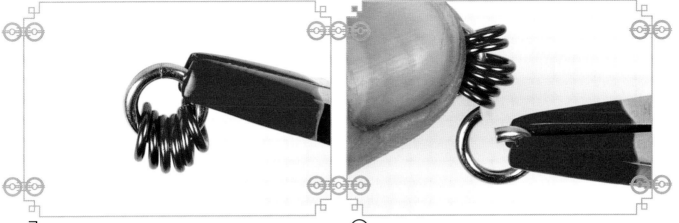

1 To prepare, close the small rings and open the large rings (see Closing Jump Rings on pages 20–25 and Opening Jump Rings on pages 26–27).

Use an open large copper ring to scoop 4 seafoam and 2 gunmetal closed enameled copper rings (see Learn to Scoop on page 28). Close the open ring.

2 Double the copper ring by taking a new open copper ring and weaving it through the same 6 closed small rings.

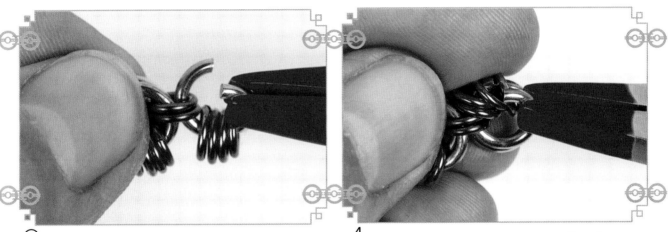

3 Using a new open large copper ring, scoop 4 seafoam rings, then weave the open copper ring through the 2 gunmetal rings from Step 1. Close the copper ring.

4 To double the copper ring added in Step 3, use a new open copper ring to go through all 6 small rings that the ring from Step 3 went through. Most people find it easier to go through the 2 gunmetal ones first because they are tighter and more fixed in place, and then the 4 seafoam rings. Close the copper ring.

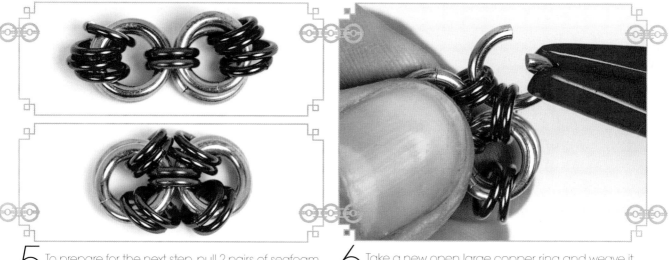

5 To prepare for the next step, pull 2 pairs of seafoam rings—1 pair from each copper unit—up toward each other. Use a wire piece to move the rings if it helps.

6 Take a new open large copper ring and weave it through those 2 sets of small seafoam rings. You'll go through 4 rings total. Close the ring.

7 Double the last ring by going through all 4 small rings with a new large ring.

8 On the other side of the weave, pull the remaining 4 hanging seafoam rings toward one another, then go through them with a new copper ring. Before closing the large ring, add the earwire. The ring that connects to the earwire is not doubled. Normally, it would be doubled, but the loop on most earwires is not large enough to accommodate 2 thick 16 gauge rings.

Once the last large ring is closed, you're done with one earring! Repeat Steps 1–8 to create the second earring.

You can easily vary one or all of the colors in this weave to suit your tastes.

Japanese Cross Earrings Variations

Making a few tiny changes, such as swapping ring sizes or adding beads, makes a world of difference in these variations. Try each one for a completely new look!

Mid-length project

MATERIALS LIST

14 small jump rings: E19 silver—19 gauge, 9/64" (3.6mm)

20 tiny jump rings: B20 anodized niobium—20 gauge, 3/32" (2.4mm)

2 earwires

2 4mm crystal bicone beads

2 silver ball headpins, at least 1¼" (3.2cm) long

TOOLS

2 pairs of small flat-nose pliers

1 wire cutter

small piece of wire (optional)

BASE METAL RING SUBSTITUTIONS

Small rings: F20—20 gauge, 5/32" (4.0mm)

Tiny rings: B20—20 gauge, 3/32" (2.4mm)

Mini Japanese Cross Earrings

The pattern here is almost identical to the Japanese Cross: the only differences are that the ring connecting to the earwire is doubled in this mini version, while the ring connecting to the crystal is not—it is a single ring. Using smaller rings does make this pair of earrings more challenging.

Mid-length project

Long project

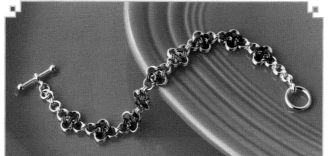

Doubled Mini Japanese Cross Earrings

This variation uses additional tiny sterling silver rings (the same sizes as the tiny niobium rings) to link multiple crosses together.

Japanese Cross Bracelet

You don't have to stop at linking just two components together. Keep going until you have enough for a bracelet or even a necklace!

Japanese Cross Pendant

 *intermediate*

MATERIALS LIST

8 large jump rings: T18 aluminum— 18 gauge, 3/8" (9.5mm)

19 small jump rings: D18 aluminum— 18 gauge, 1/8" (3.2mm)

44 small jump rings: D20 enameled copper—20 gauge, 1/8" (3.2mm)

16 color green

16 color gunmetal

8 color amber

4 color lime

pendant bail

TOOLS

2 pairs of flat-nose pliers

2 pairs of chain-nose or thin-jaw pliers (optional; use if your flat-nose pliers are too big to easily close the small rings)

PRECIOUS METAL RING SUBSTITUTIONS

Large rings: T17—17 gauge, 3/8" (9.5mm)

Small rings: D17—17 gauge, 1/8" (3.2mm)

Small rings: D20—20 gauge, 1/8" (3.2mm)*

*Pendant may be loose if niobium rings are used for the small rings.

Take the Japanese Cross weave, vary the ring size slightly and fold the weave in on itself, and you've got a whole new look. You can use a single color if that's your preference, or multiple colors for a more intricate look. These instructions show you how to weave the pendant from the inside out.

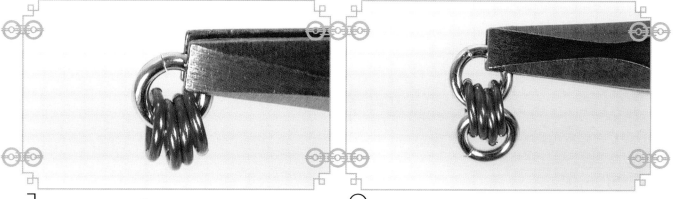

1. To prepare for this weave, open the amber jump rings and 8 gunmetal rings. Close the remaining enameled copper jump rings (see Closing Jump Rings on pages 20–25 and Opening Jump Rings on pages 26–27). Open the small and large aluminum rings.

With an open small aluminum ring, scoop up 4 lime jump rings (see Learn to Scoop on page 28). Close the aluminum ring.

2. Double the small aluminum ring by going through the same 4 small rings with a new aluminum ring. Close that ring.

3. With a new small aluminum ring, scoop up 4 small green rings and go through 1 of the lime rings. Close the aluminum ring.

4. Double the aluminum ring from Step 3 with a new small aluminum ring.

5. Separate the green rings from Step 3 into 2 groups of 2. Add an amber ring directly onto the doubled aluminum rings from Steps 3–4, between the green groups (there should be 2 green rings on each side of the amber ring). Close the amber ring.

6. Double the amber ring with a new amber ring and close it.

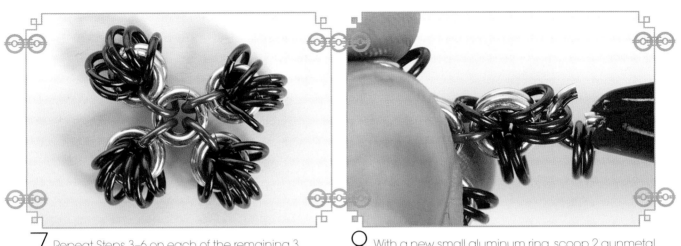

7 Repeat Steps 3–6 on each of the remaining 3 lime rings.

8 With a new small aluminum ring, scoop 2 gunmetal rings and weave through 2 of the amber rings. Close the aluminum ring.

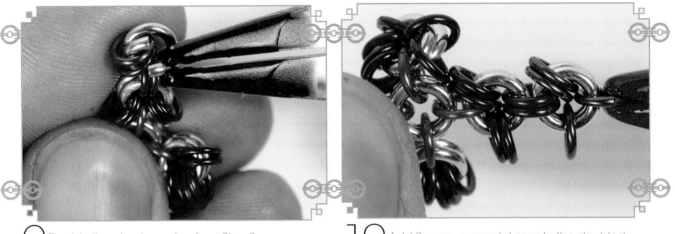

9 Double the aluminum ring from Step 8.

10 Add 2 more gunmetal rings to the doubled aluminum rings and close. You should now have 4 gunmetal rings on the small aluminum rings. (These rings were not scooped in Step 8 because it is difficult to squeeze in and close the doubled ring in Step 9.)

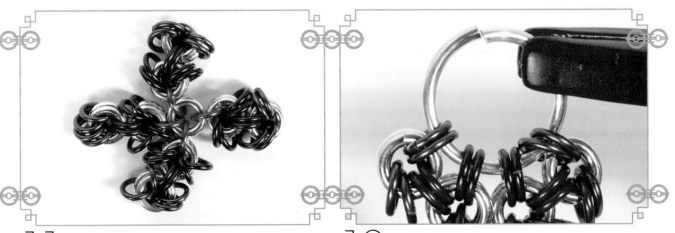

11 Repeat Steps 8–10 all the way around the piece.

12 With an open large aluminum ring, weave through 8 small enameled copper rings—2 gunmetal, 4 green and 2 gunmetal. Close the large aluminum ring.

13 Double the large ring from Step 12.

14 Repeat Steps 12-13 all the way around the piece.

15 With the final small aluminum jump ring, connect the pendant bail to a pair of large aluminum rings.

To make a pendant that is uniquely yours, vary the colors you use, or even the number of colors you use. For a special touch, you can also wrap crystal drop beads using the Wire Wrap technique on pages 32–34. Use a tiny jump ring to connect one wrapped bead to each of the 3 lower sets of large rings.

Reversible Japanese Lace Bracelet

intermediate

MATERIALS LIST FOR A 7 ¼" (18.4CM) BRACELET

60 large jump rings: L18 anodized aluminum—18 gauge, 1/4" (6.4mm)

30 color brown

30 color red

4 medium jump rings: H18 anodized aluminum—18 gauge, 3/16" (4.8mm)

2 color brown

2 color red

130 small jump rings: D20 enameled copper, color non-tarnish gold—20 gauge, 1/8" (3.2mm)

8 tiny clasp jump rings: D18 brass—18 gauge, 1/8" (3.2mm)

toggle clasp

TOOLS

2 pairs of thin-jawed flat-nose pliers

small piece of wire (optional)

PRECIOUS METAL RING SUBSTITUTIONS

Large rings: L17—17 gauge, 1/4" (6.4mm)

Small rings: D20—20 gauge, 1/8" (3.2mm)

This bracelet is made using the classic Japanese 12-in-2 weave, which means that every two (horizontal) rings are connected to twelve (vertical) rings. Since this bracelet only has two rows, the doubled rings are only connected to eight small rings—if there were a third row, you would indeed have 12-in-2. Because all of the rings are doubled, this weave is a perfect candidate for a reversible color pattern. The intricate lace-like pattern is not too difficult to learn, but closing all those small rings is definitely time-consuming.

1 Before you begin weaving, close the small jump rings and open the medium and large rings (see Closing Jump Rings on pages 20–25 and Opening Jump Rings on pages 26–27).

With an open large brown ring, scoop up 8 small rings (see Learn to Scoop on page 28). Close the large ring.

2 Add an open large red ring through the same 8 small rings, then close the large red ring. If you'd like, add a piece of wire through the 2 large rings to designate your starting point. Tie the wire piece tight enough so the 8 small rings won't slide around through the wire loop.

3 Scoop 6 small closed rings with a new open brown ring. Before closing the brown ring, weave it through 2 of the small closed rings from Step 1.

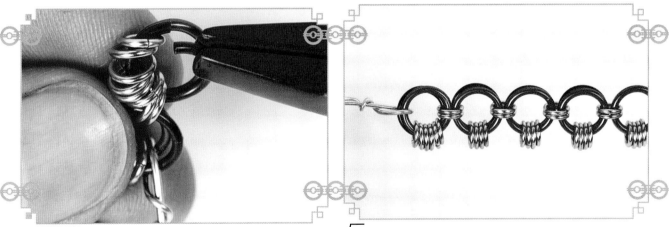

4 Weave a new open red ring through the same 8 rings as the brown ring in Step 3—the 6 small scooped rings and the 2 small rings connecting to the first unit. Make sure that you're adding the ring on the correct side of the weave to maintain the color scheme of brown on one side, red on the reverse.

5 Repeat Steps 3–4 until your piece is as long as you'd like minus approximately 1½" (3.8cm) for the clasp. Make sure all the brown rings are on one side of the weave, and all the red rings are on the other. Each pair of brown/red rings should have 4 small hanging rings (the end sets each have 6 hanging rings).

6 You'll now begin the second row of the weave. With an open brown ring, scoop 4 small closed rings, then go through 4 small hanging rings from the first row. Ignore the first 4 small hanging rings on the first large ring; guide the open brown ring through the last 2 small rings on the first set of large rings and through the first 2 small rings on the second set of large rings. Close the brown ring.

7 With a red ring, double the brown ring you added in Step 6 and close. The new ring goes through the same 8 small rings. To visualize where the next set of large rings go, it can be helpful to lay the piece flat.

8 Scoop 2 small rings with a new open brown ring, then go through 6 small rings: 2 from the first ring in the second row and 4 hanging rings from the first row, divided into 2 groups of 2, just like in Step 6. Close the brown ring. Double this ring with a new red ring.

9 Repeat Step 8 until you reach the end of your piece. The last set of large rings only go through 2 hanging rings from Row 1. At the end of your piece you should have 4 small hanging rings (2 from each row).

You could attach the clasp directly onto the last set of rings from either row; however, the piece may look lopsided because the clasp is not centered. The following steps show you how to taper your ends.

10 Scoop 2 small closed rings onto a medium brown ring. Weave the brown ring through the 4 small hanging rings on the end. Close the medium ring. Double the medium brown ring with a medium red ring as you have with the large rings throughout the weave.

11   Now the medium ring has hanging rings, but the large set of rings at the end doesn't. Add 2 new small rings to the last large set.

Open a tiny brass ring and go through the 4 small hanging rings at the end. Double the brass ring.

12   With a new tiny brass ring, attach your clasp to the doubled brass rings.

13   Repeat Steps 10–11 at the opposite end of the weave. The large set of rings should already have the extra 2 small hanging rings, so you don't need to add another set.

Connect the second half of the clasp with a series of tiny brass rings.

Just because this bracelet can be reversible doesn't mean it has to be! If you'd prefer the weave to look the same on each side, you'll have the added bonus of an easier weave because you don't have to pay attention to color placement.

3-Row Variation

You can easily create a 3-row version of the *Reversible Japanese Lace Bracelet*. In this variation, Row 1 is the center row. Work Steps 1–9, then add 4 small hanging rings to the empty side of each large ring in Row 1. Repeat Steps 6–9 on the other side of Row 1 to create a third row. Attach your clasp to the ends of Row 1 to finish the bracelet.

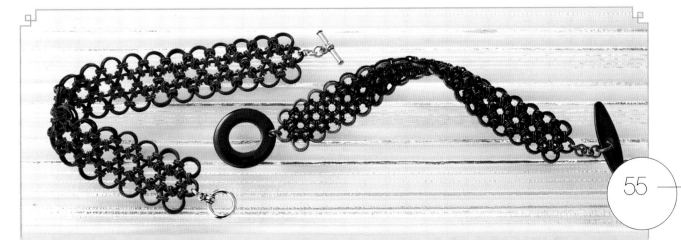

Japanese Diamond Earrings

intermediate

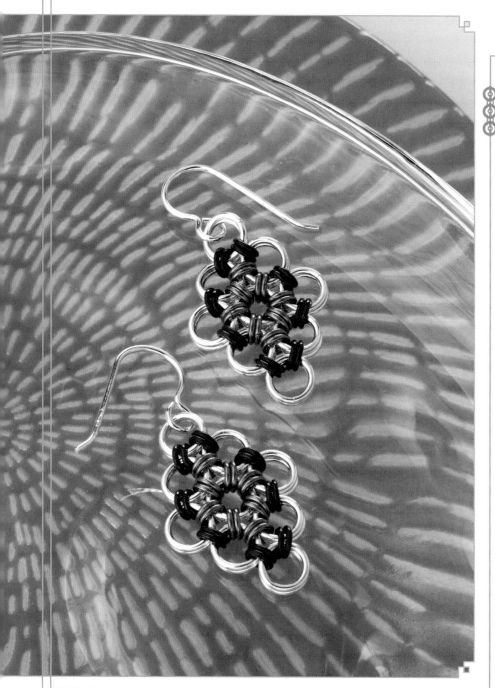

Mid-length project

MATERIALS LIST

36 medium jump rings: G19
sterling—19 gauge, 11/64" (4.4mm)

64 tiny jump rings: B20 anodized
niobium—20 gauge, 3/32" (2.4mm)

32 color brown

32 color green

2 earwires

TOOLS

2 pairs of flat-nose pliers with narrow
jaws, or 2 pairs of chain-nose pliers

BASE METAL RING
SUBSTITUTIONS

Medium rings: H18—18 gauge, 3/16"
(4.8mm)

Tiny rings: D20—20 gauge 1/8"
(3.2mm)

The base metal piece will be slightly
larger than the sterling/niobium
combination shown here.

The pattern is basic, but working with tiny rings is tricky! With 50 jump rings
per earring, this project takes a bit of time. The end result is well worth it,
however—a svelte pair of earrings that can be color-customized to match
your favorite outfit.

1 To prepare, open the medium rings. Close 16 of the brown rings, and open the other 16. Close 24 of the green rings, and open the remaining 8 (see Closing Jump Rings on pages 20–25 and Opening Jump Rings on pages 26–27).
  Scoop 8 tiny green rings with a medium ring, then close the medium ring (see Learn to Scoop on page 28).

2 Double the medium ring with a new medium ring. Add another open tiny green ring to the large rings and close.

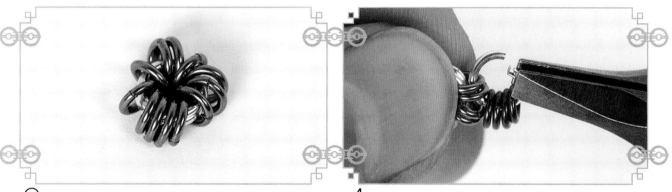

3 To finish the center of the pattern, add 3 more open tiny green rings to the doubled medium rings, closing each after it is added. (The reason you don't begin with all 12 green rings on the medium ring in Step 1 is that with all those small rings you wouldn't have enough room to get your pliers in there to close the medium ring!)

4 Scoop 4 closed brown rings onto a medium ring and go through 2 of the hanging green rings. Close this medium ring, then double it with another medium ring. When adding the second ring it is usually easier to come up through the green rings first, and as you continue moving the ring, use the fingers of your non-dominant hand to slide the brown rings onto the open medium ring. When you're through all 6 rings, close the second medium ring.

5 You will now start working your way around the center, going through two pairs of adjacent hanging tiny rings—one pair from the previous set of medium rings, and one pair from the center. With a new medium ring, scoop up 2 green rings. Weave the medium ring through 2 brown rings and 2 green rings. Close the medium ring and double it.

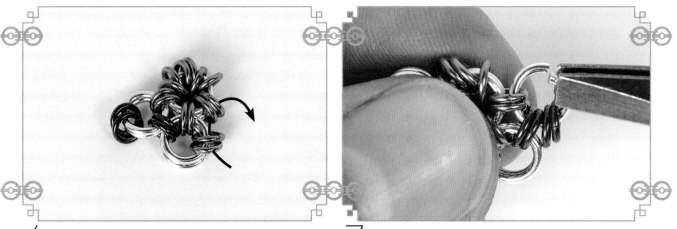

6 Next, scoop 2 brown rings onto a new medium ring and go through the 2 green hanging rings from the previous medium ring and 2 green rings from the center. Close the medium ring and double it.

7 Scoop 2 more brown rings onto a new medium ring and go through the 2 brown rings on the previous medium ring and the next 2 green rings in the center. Close the medium ring and double it.

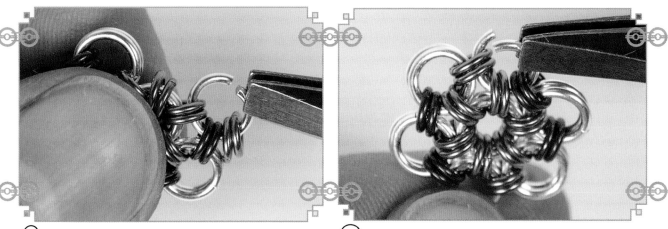

8 Continue around the center ring: Scoop 2 green rings onto a new medium ring and go through the 2 brown rings on the previous medium ring and the next 2 green rings in the center. Close this medium ring and then double it.

9 With a new medium ring, go through the remaining 6 hanging rings—2 green rings from the previous medium ring, 2 green rings from the center and the 2 free brown rings on the first medium ring from Step 4. Do not add any more tiny rings to this medium ring.

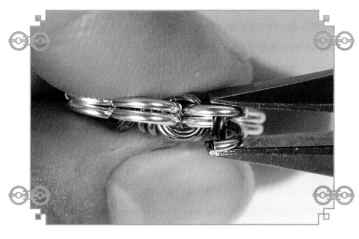

10 Double the ring from Step 9. Be careful not to open it too wide, or you'll have difficulty closing the ring. To help close the ring, you can sandwich it between your pliers as shown, and then fine-tune the closure as you normally would with two pliers. (Before sandwiching, be sure to first spin the first ring around so the closure is hidden on the inside of the weave.)

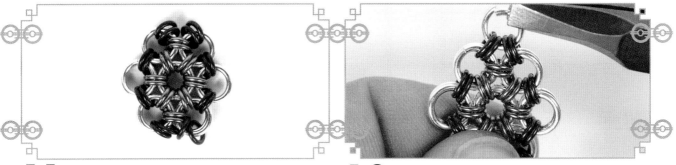

11 Add 2 open brown rings to each set of medium rings that is currently only connected to 2 brown rings. The brown rings now form a diamond outline.

12 Go through 4 adjacent hanging brown rings with a new medium ring and close it. Double that ring.

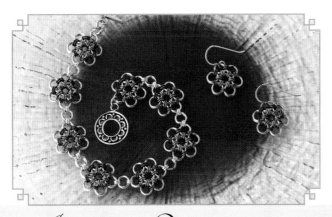

13 Repeat Step 12 on the other side of the weave, but add the earwire before closing the medium rings.

Try this weave pattern in your favorite colors, or for an even more elegant pair of earrings, enhance the pattern with beads and additional rings. The pair on the right uses 4mm beads and bicone crystals, and (lots) more B20 sterling and niobium rings.

Japanese Diamond Flower Variations

 intermediate  Long project

After working Steps 1–9, your piece resembles a flower. You can use units like these as earrings, or you can connect multiple flowers together for a bracelet or necklace. The Flower unit works best if the outer colors are all one color, rather than multiple colors.

Japanese Diamond Pendant

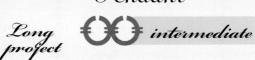 intermediate  Quick project

To make a pendant to match your earrings, follow Steps 1–12, but then at Step 13 add a pendant bail instead of an earwire. This pendant combines several colors to create a color fade. (If you are creating a color fade, it is easier to weave across the diamond, row by row, rather than working from the center. Follow the techniques for the *Reversible Japanese Lace Bracelet* on page 52 to work row-by-row.)

Japanese Diamond Ring

expert

Mid-length project

MATERIALS LIST

FOR THE DIAMOND

7 thick medium jump rings: F18
stainless steel—18 gauge, 5/32"
(4.0mm)

11 thin medium jump rings: F20
stainless steel—20 gauge, 5/32"
(4.0mm)

32 tiny jump rings: B22 anodized
titanium—22 gauge, 3/32" (2.4mm)

16 color brown

16 color pink

FOR THE BAND

12–16 small jump rings: C20 stainless
steel—20 gauge, 7/64" (2.8mm)

7–10 stainless steel jump rings in sizes
F18 (18 gauge, 5/32" [4.0mm]) to I18
(18 gauge, 13/64" [5.2mm]) (see Ring
Sizing below)

TOOLS

2 pairs of flat-nose pliers strong
enough to work with 18 gauge steel

2 smaller pairs of thin-jawed flat-nose
pliers to work with the small and tiny
rings (optional)

RING SIZING

*The sizing for finger rings is tough! The first
step you can take in sizing is to change the
number of rings in your band. However, if
your ring is too big or too small, but removing or adding an 18 gauge ring would alter
the size too much, then try substituting one
or two of those rings with another 18 gauge
ring that is slightly smaller or slightly larger.
Play around until the ring fits perfectly.*

A finger ring must withstand a great deal of stress, not only from finger
movements but also from the changes in the size of the finger itself that
occur during temperature fluctuations, especially on hot, humid days.
Stainless steel and titanium are two of the strongest metals and perfect
for use in finger rings, but working with them is tough, hence the expert
rating for this project! The pattern is basically the same as the Japanese
Diamond Earrings, except different sizes of rings need to be used for the
horizontal rings in order to keep the weave stable—flexible enough to
be comfortable, but not overly loose.

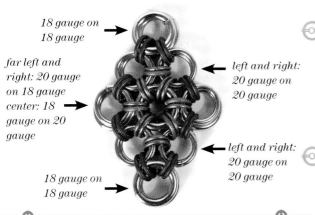

18 gauge on
18 gauge

*far left and
right: 20 gauge
on 18 gauge
center: 18
gauge on 20
gauge*

*left and right:
20 gauge on
20 gauge*

*left and right:
20 gauge on
20 gauge*

18 gauge on
18 gauge

TO CREATE THE DIAMOND SHAPE

Weave a Japanese Diamond as outlined on pages 57–59, but use horizontal ring sizes shown in the diagram above. Note that the middle row is unusual; the doubled rings are not the same size. Instead, they are staggered so the thin and thick rings alternate positions.

1 Prepare the band rings by closing the small rings and opening the 18 gauge rings (see Closing Tough Rings on page 25).

Add 2 small rings to each side of the center row of the diamond.

2 With an 18 gauge ring, scoop 2 small rings and go through a set of small rings added in Step 1. Close the 18 gauge ring.

3 Repeat Step 2 to lengthen the band.

4 Once the band is the length you desire, join it to the other side of the ring. The last 18 gauge ring goes through the 2 previous small rings, plus the other 2 small rings you added in Step 1.

Horizontal Diamond Ring

You can create a horizontal or vertical ring, depending on where you attach the connecting rings in Step 1. And, as always, you can also create your favorite color effect, including subtle color fades.

Japanese Diamond Bracelet

 *expert*

MATERIALS LIST FOR A 7" (17.8CM) BRACELET

146 medium jump rings: G19 sterling—19 gauge, 11/64" (4.4mm)

48 small jump rings: D19 sterling—19 gauge, 1/8" (3.2mm)

236 tiny jump rings: B20 sterling—20 gauge, 3/32" (2.4mm)

192 tiny jump rings: B20 anodized niobium—20 gauge, 3/32" (2.4mm)

> 96 color midnight blue

> 96 color lime

32 tiny clasp rings: B20 sterling—20 gauge, 3/32" (2.4mm)

3-strand slide clasp

TOOLS

2 pairs of flat-nose pliers

small piece of wire (optional)

BASE METAL RING SUBSTITUTIONS

Medium rings: H18—18 gauge, 3/16" (4.8mm)

Small rings: F18—18 gauge, 5/32" (4.0mm)

Tiny rings: D20—20 gauge 1/8" (3.2mm)

The base metal piece will be slightly larger than the sterling/niobium combination shown here (which also makes it a bit easier).

This stunning bracelet combines the Japanese Diamond pattern with the *Reversible Japanese Lace Bracelet* weave. Working with tiny rings is difficult, and getting the colors to line up requires great attention to detail, which is why this is an expert-level project. You should first be fluent with Japanese Lace before attempting this weave.

This piece is significantly easier if you use one color for the outer diamond outlines. However, the "argyle sock" pattern shown here is a favorite of my customers. Since the argyle pattern is trickier, I'm demonstrating it here to make it easier for you to tackle on your own. If your diamond outlines just use one color (like the color variations shown on page 67), then you simply use one color instead of the lime and midnight rings shown here.

Stage 1: Weave Row 1 with 4 Hanging Rings

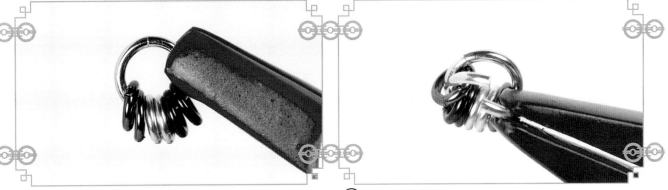

1 Open all medium rings before starting. To prepare for Stage 1, close 96 tiny silver rings, 48 tiny midnight blue rings and 2 lime rings (see Closing Jump Rings on pages 20–25 and Opening Jump Rings on pages 26–27).

Put 4 tiny outer rings (2 lime and 2 midnight blue) and 2 tiny inner (silver) rings on a medium ring and close the jump ring.

2 Double the medium ring with a new medium ring and close.

3 Scoop 6 tiny inner rings (silver for the argyle sock pattern) on a new medium ring, and weave it through the 2 tiny inner (silver) rings from the first unit and close (see Learn to Scoop on page 28). Double this ring. Please note: If you are using colored rings for the inner diamond, remember to use that color each time an "inner" ring is called for.

4 Continue the pattern of Japanese Lace for the full length of your bracelet: With a medium ring, scoop 6 tiny rings (2 outer [midnight blue], 2 inner [silver], 2 outer [midnight blue]) and go through the middle set of inner (silver) rings from the previous step. Double the medium ring. Then scoop 6 tiny inner (silver) rings and go through the inner (silver) rings from the previous step. Repeat until your piece is as long as you need it to be (minus ½" [1.3cm] for the clasp).

Finish Stage 1 with 2 outer (midnight blue) hanging rings.

Stage 2: Add Extra Hanging Rings to Complete Row 1

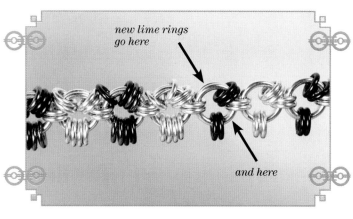

new lime rings go here

and here

5 To prepare, open 46 tiny lime rings and 48 tiny silver rings. For this step of the weave, you will go through the entire piece and add extra hanging rings.

On the inner (silver) color units, add 4 more inner (silver) color rings, 2 on each side of the row. There will now be a total of 8 hanging rings on these units, 4 on each side of the row.

For the "argyle sock" units, add 4 outer (lime) color rings to each unit. The lime rings should alternate with the midnight blue rings within a single unit. The next "argyle sock" unit over will be a mirror image of the first. This is how the zigzag effect is achieved.

Add 2 lime rings (instead of 4) to the end unit.

Stage 3: Weave the Outer Rows

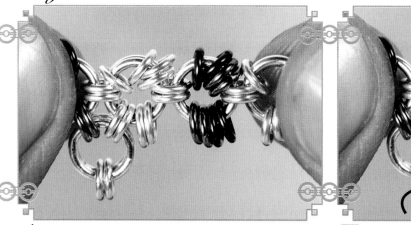

6 Close 48 tiny inner rings (silver) and 44 tiny connector rings (for this pattern, also silver).

Your first ring will go through the first 4 hanging rings, just like the regular Japanese Lace (see page 54, Step 6). With a new medium ring, scoop up 2 inner (silver) color rings and go through those first 4 hanging rings. Close the medium ring, and make sure your piece looks like the photo above. Double the newly added medium ring with another medium ring.

If your pliers aren't small enough, you might need to skip the pre-closing stage mentioned above. Instead, just add the medium rings without scooping up the closed tiny rings, then add the tiny rings to the medium rings.

7 Just like regular Japanese Lace, your next ring goes through the hanging rings from the newly added medium rings, plus the next 4 hanging rings from Row 1. You'll scoop 2 connector (silver) tiny rings this time.

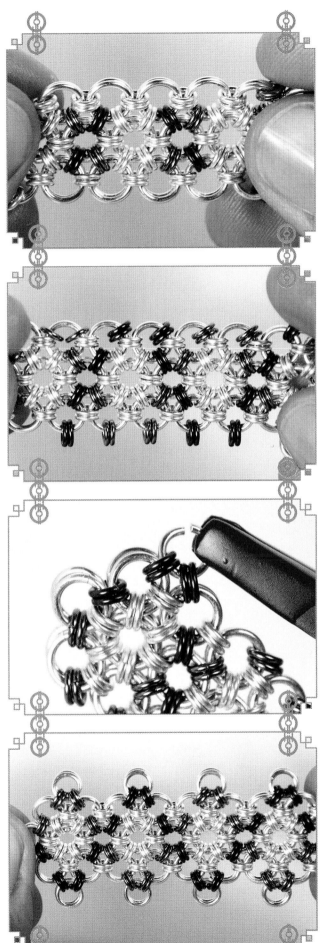

8 Continue the Japanese Lace pattern all the way to the end, then flip the weave over to do the same thing on the other side. Alternate inner color rings with connector color rings (in this case, inner color and connector color rings are silver, so no alternation is needed; however, if you're creating a piece like the variations shown on page 67, you'll alternate colors).

Stage 4: Add the Hanging Rings

9 Open 96 outer color rings (for this pattern, 48 lime and 48 midnight blue).
  Work your way down the weave, adding 2 tiny outer color hanging rings on each set of medium rings in the outer rows. For the "argyle sock" pattern shown here, match the color to the tiny rings that are already on that unit (connecting to Row 1, the center row).

Stage 5: Create the Edging

10 Open all 48 small rings.
  Join the first two sets of hanging rings with a small ring and close. Double this small ring.

11 Repeat Step 10 on the other side of the weave, then continue the pattern along the length of both sides of the entire piece.

12 Open the 32 tiny clasp rings. Add 2 tiny clasp rings to each of the three sets of medium rings at the end of the piece.

13 Add a new tiny ring going through 1 of the hanging rings attached to the center medium ring, and through the adjacent 2 hanging rings from the end. Double this ring. (This is a tight squeeze! However, the doubling is important for strength.)

14 Repeat Step 13 on the other side of the center.

15 With a new tiny ring, attach the clasp to the end of the weave. You may need to rest the piece against the pad of your finger for leverage when you go through. Close this ring.

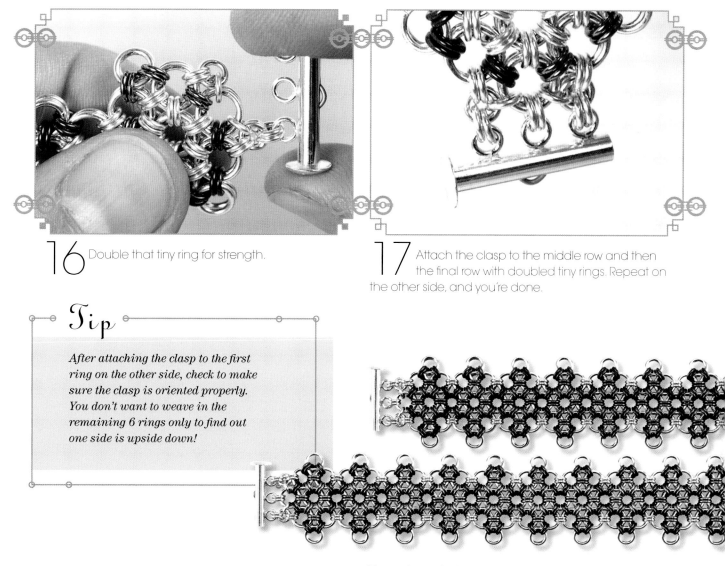

16 Double that tiny ring for strength.

17 Attach the clasp to the middle row and then the final row with doubled tiny rings. Repeat on the other side, and you're done.

Tip

After attaching the clasp to the first ring on the other side, check to make sure the clasp is oriented properly. You don't want to weave in the remaining 6 rings only to find out one side is upside down!

These color variations, with one inner color and one outer color, don't take as much attention to weave as the argyle pattern, and certainly have their own charm as well.

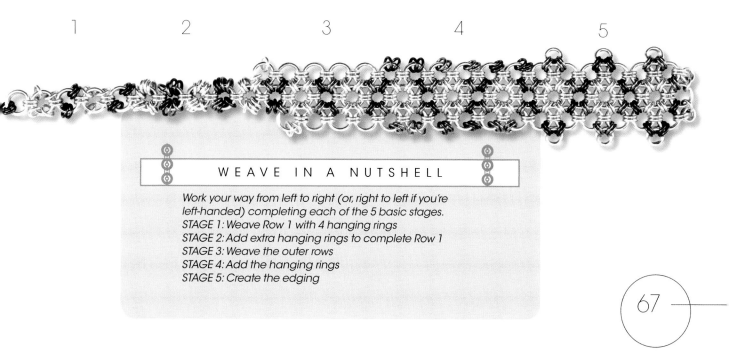

1   2   3   4   5

WEAVE IN A NUTSHELL

Work your way from left to right (or, right to left if you're left-handed) completing each of the 5 basic stages.
STAGE 1: Weave Row 1 with 4 hanging rings
STAGE 2: Add extra hanging rings to complete Row 1
STAGE 3: Weave the outer rows
STAGE 4: Add the hanging rings
STAGE 5: Create the edging

Byzantine

Byzantine (pronounced BIZ-en-teen or BYE-zen-teen) belongs to the European family of weaves and is one of the most famous chain mail jewelry patterns. This weave is often one of the first weaves a new student learns. The European family encompasses too many weaves to fit in a single chapter, so I've chosen Byzantine as the family's representative because it's so well known and also because the myriad of ways Byzantine can be modified is mind-boggling. When I began exploring the variations I truly became enthralled with this pattern.

Though it is not immediately obvious, Byzantine is based on the most famous chain mail pattern of all: the European 4-in-1 weave, seen in most historical chain link shirts from Europe. If you take a small 3-row segment of such a shirt, fold it in on itself and zip it up with a new row of rings, you'd create the Box weave (featured on page 70). It's a little tricky to make Box that way, though, so the instructions demonstrate a much easier method!

Looking at the rings on one side of the Box weave, you'll notice that they are all angled in the same direction, and they are attached to rings on either side that are angled in the opposite direction. That is a typical characteristic of a European family weave, and it creates a completely different look from the strict perpendicular connections of the Japanese family.

Once you've gotten the hang of the Box weave, a few simple changes in ring size will yield fantastic results (the *Ripple Necklace and Earrings* on page 75). Or, jump right into the *Basic Byzantine Necklace* (page 76), a series of Box units linked with connector rings.

After you've conquered the *Basic Byzantine Necklace*, you're ready to tackle any other project in this chapter; they are all different takes on the basic Byzantine unit. The final project (the *Floating Bead Pendant* on page 90) combines Byzantine with Japanese. The horizontal connector rings in Byzantine lend themselves well to Japanese-style expansions, and the variations you can create by combining these two patterns are endless.

On a historical note, some say this pattern dates back to the late Middle Ages, while others claim there is evidence of Byzantine found all over the world dating back more than 2,000 years. Because the weave is a variation of European 4-in-1, it's quite possible that the Byzantine chain was developed shortly after the European 4-in-1 weave came into popular use in armor. I can imagine a blacksmith's apprentice lollygagging around, absentmindedly fiddling with a patch of European 4-in-1, eventually inventing the Byzantine weave. An alternate name for this weave is Idiot's Delight—I'll let you use your imagination about where that name came from!

Box Chain Bracelet

beginner

Mid-length project

MATERIALS LIST FOR A 7¼" (18.4CM) BRACELET

142 medium jump rings: H18 anodized niobium—18 gauge, 3/16" (4.8mm)

71 mixed icy blue colors

71 mixed brown colors

2–4 tiny clasp rings: D18 copper—18 gauge, 1/8" (3.2mm)

2 small clasp rings: F18 copper—18 gauge, 5/32" (4.0mm)

toggle clasp

TOOLS

2 pairs of flat-nose pliers

1–2 pieces of wire

BASE METAL RING SUBSTITUTIONS

J18—18 gauge, 7/32" (5.6mm)

ALTERNATE SMALLER PRECIOUS AND BASE METAL SIZES

F20—20 gauge, 5/32" (4.0mm)

Mastering Box weave (also known as Inca Puño and Queen's Maille) is crucial for progressing to Byzantine. The Box chain is exactly that: a rectangular shape created by circular jump rings. Everything in this weave is doubled: Two sides of the Box are built up by two jump rings, then another two sides are attached and folded back so that all rings are in the same plane. The flip step can be a bit tricky, but once you get the hang of it, this is one of the easiest and most soothing weaves. I highly recommend learning Box in two colors.

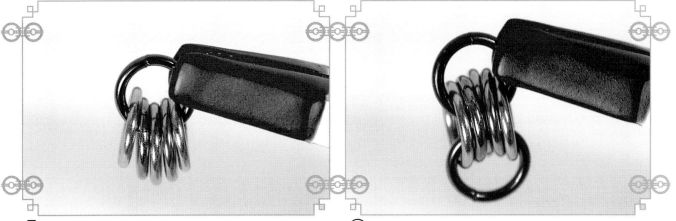

1 To prepare for this weave, open all the brown jump rings; close 5 of the icy blue jump rings, and open the rest (see Closing Jump Rings on pages 20–25 and Opening Jump Rings on pages 26–27).

With an open brown ring, scoop 5 closed icy blue rings, then close the open ring (see Learn to Scoop on page 28).

2 Add another open brown ring through the same 5 closed blue rings, and close that ring.

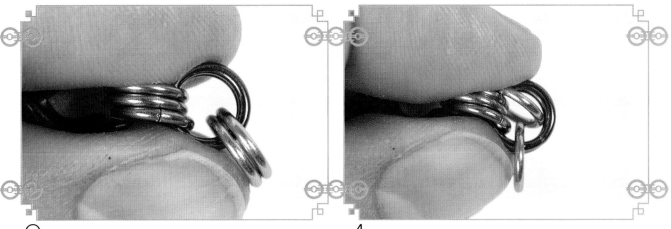

3 Separate the 5 blue rings into a group of 2 and a group of 3. With a small piece of wire, go through the group of 3 and twist the wire together to mark your starting point.

Hold the 3 rings between the thumb and index finger of your non-dominant hand as shown.

4 Flip the 2 end rings back; tuck 1 of them under your index finger.

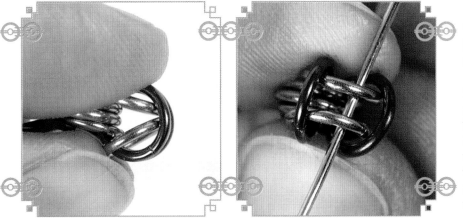

5 Tuck the other under your thumb. This folding has created your first Box unit, but it is not yet stable until we add more rings.

The positioning of the rings is very important, so stop to check that your piece looks like the picture at far left from the sides and the picture at near left from the top (minus the piece of wire inserted in the weave). Both of the tucked rings should be firmly tucked and not easily jostled when you add the new ring in Step 7.

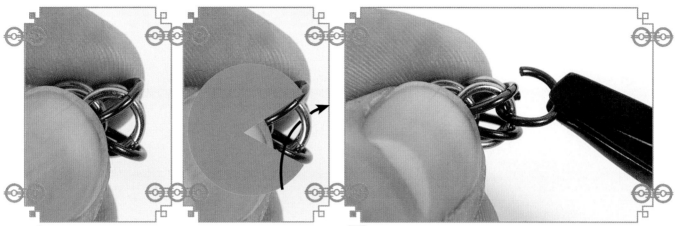

6 Rotate your palm to bring the flipped rings horizontal. See the rings that look like an old-school video game mouth? Your next rings go through that "mouth."

7 Add a new open ring (brown) through the mouth, and close. Note that the new ring hooks onto the rings that you flipped (blue) back in Steps 4–5. As you're closing, keep a good eye on the ring, because your next ring needs to go right next to it.

Tip

If you have trouble getting the ring through in Step 7, use a gently curved wire piece to go through the mouth first. Once you're sure the wire is in the right spot, you can even twist tie it together so it really holds your place while you add the rings for Steps 7–9.

8 Double the ring you added in the last step. Again, keep an eye on the ring as you close. At this stage, the weave is not yet stable, and the flipped-back rings could flop back into their original position!

9 Add a new open ring (blue) through the doubled rings you just added (brown) and close. Double that ring and close. Keep holding it in your pliers after you've closed the ring.

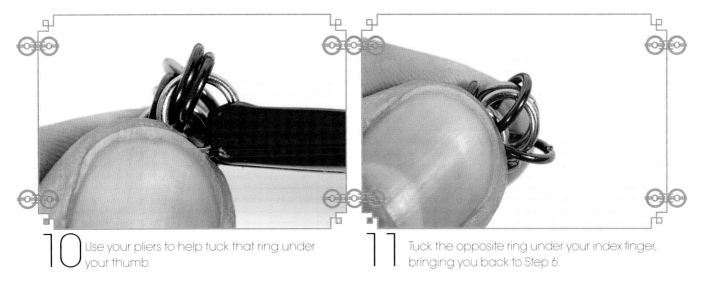

10 Use your pliers to help tuck that ring under your thumb.

11 Tuck the opposite ring under your index finger, bringing you back to Step 6.

12 Repeat Steps 7–9 until your piece is the length you desire (see Speedweaving Box Chain on page 74). To add a clasp to your piece, add 3 brown rings through the mouth, instead of just 2 as you normally would.

With a small clasp ring, go through the 3 rings, and add the toggle.

13 On the other side, remove your starting wire, and add the bar part of the toggle. You'll need to first build a small chain with the tiny rings in order to give the bar enough slack to pull through the toggle.

A variety of color and size variations work for this weave, making it a good choice for both men and women. The stainless steel version shown above at left is a favorite among my male customers. A bit of pre-planning can lead to gorgeous variations. With the ring size used here, there are about 5½ units of Box per inch (about 2¼ per centimeter), which means that a typical bracelet 7" (17.8cm) in length— not including clasp—would have about 38 units. Once you know how many units of Box you need to fit your wrist (again, don't forget to take the clasp into account!) you can create color fade patterns. For the rainbow variation shown above right, each of the 36 Box units is a slightly different color.

*If you get the hang of the weave
quickly, try these Speedweaving steps.*

Add 2 rings through the "mouth."

*To start, only open about 12 brown rings, which is
enough for you to get the hang of the weave. Leave
the remaining rings "raw"—straight from the bag.
When you're going through the mouth, scoop up 2
raw rings of the second color first. Close the open
ring. Before you forget, close the 2 raw rings, too.*

Add another 2 rings to the previous 2.

Double the open ring: first go through the mouth.

Flip the last 2 rings back to make a new "mouth."

*Then go through the hanging rings. Now you're
ready to flip back the rings and repeat!*

Box Chain Variations

Ripple Necklace and Earrings

 intermediate Long project

This stunning necklace is simply a Box weave that uses a different size for each unit. Spread out little piles of each ring size that you need, keeping them organized from largest to smallest. Follow the steps in Speedweaving Box Chain on page 74 using 4 rings of the same size. When you repeat the three steps, move to the next size ring, and so on. When you weave the smallest and largest units, simply do one unit and then move on to the next size. (In other words, you'll never have two large units or two small units next to one another.) Finish each end by going up to the largest size, then tapering down one size for the final unit.

The Ripple weave also works great for earrings. You'll need to add enough rings to the bottom to keep the last Box unit flipped in place (otherwise gravity will pull it down).

Mini Ripple Variation
For a more subtle Ripple, follow the pattern of small-to-large and back again, but omit the largest size ring.

MATERIALS LIST FOR A 20" (50.8CM) NECKLACE

56 jump rings: D21 sterling silver—21 gauge, 1/8" (3.2mm)

112 jump rings: E20 sterling silver—20 gauge, 9/64" (3.6mm)

112 jump rings: G19 sterling silver—19 gauge, 11/64" (4.4mm)

160 jump rings: J17 sterling silver—17 gauge, 7/32" (5.6mm)

60 jump rings: O14 sterling silver—14 gauge, 19/64" (7.5mm)

6 clasp rings: E18 sterling silver—18 gauge, 9/64" (3.6mm)

lobster claw clasp

soldered closed ring

BASE METAL RING SUBSTITUTIONS

D20—20 gauge, 1/8" (3.2mm)

F20—20 gauge, 5/32" (4.0mm)

H18—18 gauge, 3/16" (4.8mm)

J18—18 gauge, 7/32" (5.6mm)

P16—16 gauge, 5/16" (7.9mm)

Basic Byzantine Necklace

beginner

Long project

MATERIALS LIST FOR AN 18" (45.7CM) NECKLACE

216 jump rings: H18 bronze—18 gauge, 3/16" (4.8mm)

156 jump rings: H18 anodized aluminum, color black—18 gauge, 3/16" (4.8mm)

2–4 tiny clasp rings: D18 bronze—18 gauge, 1/8" (3.2mm)

clasp

TOOLS

2 pairs of flat-nose pliers (you may need sturdy pliers to work with the bronze)

PRECIOUS METAL RING SUBSTITUTIONS

H17—17 gauge, 3/16" (4.8 mm)

The Byzantine weave, also known by the names Idiot's Delight, Fool's Dilemma and Birdcage, is a classic chain mail weave. Combine anodized aluminum with bronze jump rings for a necklace that is timeless and sophisticated. If bronze is too difficult for you to manipulate, use copper or aluminum instead.

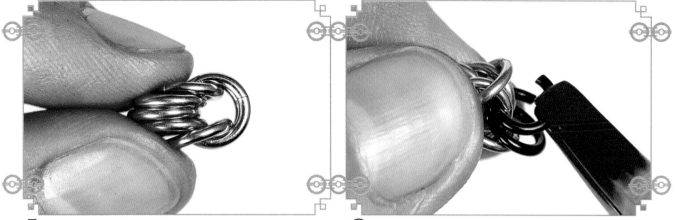

1 Start by opening all of the black jump rings. Close 107 bronze rings, and open 109 bronze rings (see Closing Jump Rings on pages 20–25 and Opening Jump Rings on pages 26–27).

Using the bronze rings, follow Steps 1-5 of the *Box Chain Bracelet* on page 71.

2 Using black rings, add 2 new rings, just as in Steps 7–8 of the *Box Chain Bracelet* on page 72.

3 Slide a third black ring into the same spot as the previous 2 black rings you added, and close. These 3 rings are "connector" rings, as they connect units of Box chain (see Step 3 on page 81 for more information).

4 Now you'll add another Box unit. With an open bronze ring, scoop up 2 closed bronze rings, and weave through the tripled black connector rings. Close the bronze ring.

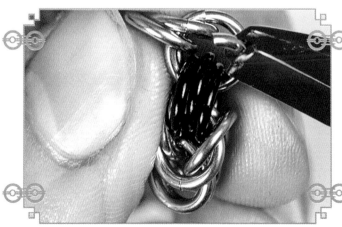

5 With a new bronze ring, double the ring you added in Step 4.

6 Flip the bronze rings back, just like in the *Box Chain Bracelet*, and add a new connector ring.

7 Add 2 more black rings for a total of 3 connector rings.

8 Repeat Steps 4–7 until your piece is the length you desire. When you reach the end, make the last set of connectors bronze instead of black.

9 Weave a new bronze ring through the final set of connectors to add your clasp. Repeat on the other side to attach the opposite end of the clasp.

WEAVE IN A NUTSHELL

Add 3 connector rings.

Add 2 sets of 2 rings, flip and repeat!

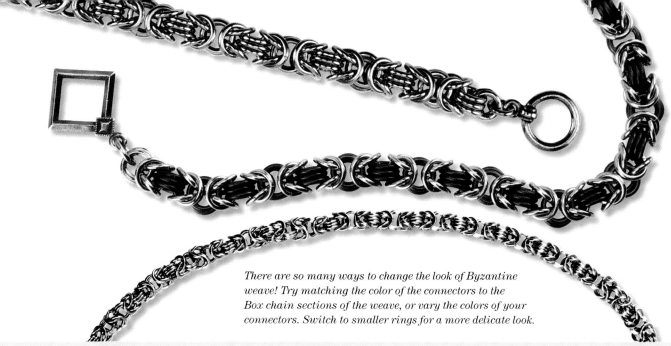

There are so many ways to change the look of Byzantine weave! Try matching the color of the connectors to the Box chain sections of the weave, or vary the colors of your connectors. Switch to smaller rings for a more delicate look.

Byzantine Weave Variations
2-Connector Byzantine and 2-and-3-Connector Byzantine

 *beginner*　　　　　　　 *Mid-length project*

The experienced chain mailer might notice that the Byzantine weave outlined on pages 76–78 looks slightly different from the traditional Byzantine pattern; the version stepped out here uses the 3-Connector method, rather than the more common 2-Connector version. I find the 3-Connector version is easier for students to learn, as the rings are larger and the weave is roomier. The aspect ratio of the rings used in a 3-Connector Byzantine is higher than the rings typically used for 2-Connector Byzantine. You can make 2-Connector Byzantine using the same ring size as 3-Connector, but the weave would be very loose. I recommend squeezing in as many connector rings as you can fit to fill out the weave. The examples shown here are 2-Connector Byzantine (earrings and bracelet on left) and 2-and-3-Connector Byzantine (bracelet on right). As the name indicates, 2-and-3-Connector Byzantine has alternating connections of 2 rings (blue in this example) and 3 rings (orange in this example).

Olivia Bracelet

intermediate

Mid-length project

MATERIALS LIST FOR A 7¼" (18.4CM) BRACELET

62 jump rings: H18 aluminum—18 gauge, 3/16" (4.8mm)

170 jump rings: H18 anodized aluminum—18 gauge, 3/16" (4.8mm)

144 color blue

26 color brown

4 tiny clasp rings: D18 aluminum—18 gauge, 1/8" (3.2mm)

2-strand slide clasp

TOOLS

2 pairs of flat-nose pliers

PRECIOUS METAL RING SUBSTITUTIONS

H17—17 gauge, 3/16" (4.8mm)

This deceptively simple weave is one of my favorites. The pattern is actually Byzantine, just flipped on its side and connected along the edges. Because the edging rings are doubled, you can use two colors to create a reversible bracelet, like the blue and brown one shown here.

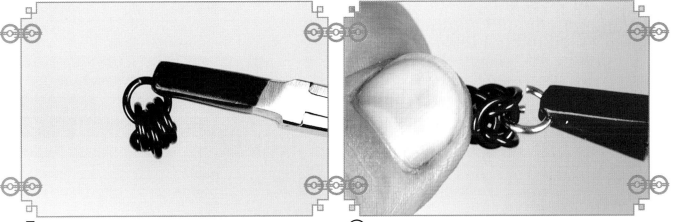

1 To prepare for weaving, close 48 blue rings. Open the remaining blue rings, and all of the brown and aluminum rings (see Closing Jump Rings on pages 20–25 and Opening Jump Rings on pages 26–27).

Scoop 4 closed blue rings with an open blue ring and close (see Learn to Scoop on page 28). Double the first ring by adding a new blue ring through the same 4 closed blue rings and close.

2 Separate the 4 scooped rings from Step 1 into 2 groups of 2, and follow Steps 4–7 from the *Box Chain Bracelet* instructions on pages 71–72 to add a new aluminum ring. Close that ring.

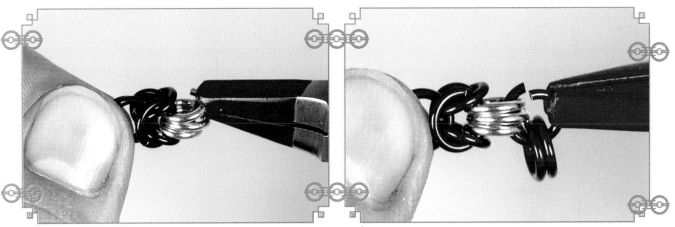

3 Add another aluminum ring adjacent to the ring added in Step 2, just as you would in Box chain. Squeeze a third aluminum ring into the same opening. This might be a tight fit! To work your way into the weave, first, aim the end of the ring into the opening. As you weave, you may need to wiggle both your hands slightly to "burrow" the jump ring through. Then double check to make sure the ring pops out in the right spot on the other side of the weave. It should glide in exactly on top of the previous aluminum ring and not cross it. Close that ring.

4 With a new open blue ring, scoop 2 closed blue rings and weave it through the triple aluminum rings. Close the blue ring. Double this ring by adding a new blue ring through the same 2 closed blue rings, plus the 3 aluminum rings. Close that ring.

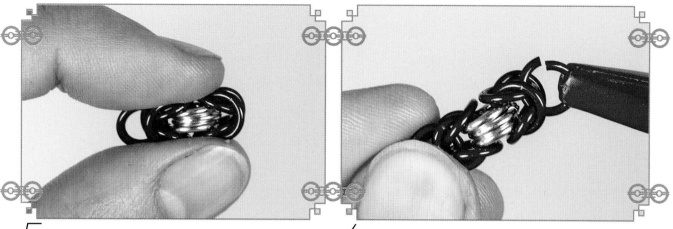

5 Flip the last 2 blue rings back, as shown in Steps 4–5 of the *Box Chain Bracelet* on page 71.

6 Add a new blue ring through the flipped rings and close.

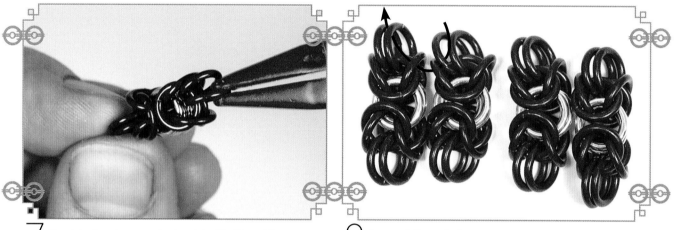

7 Double the ring you just added in Step 6 to complete your first unit.

8 Repeat Steps 1–7 to create more units. For the bracelet shown here, you need 12 units.

You'll begin to join the units together by weaving a new ring through 4 blue rings—2 from one unit, and 2 from the adjacent unit as shown by the arrow in the photo above.

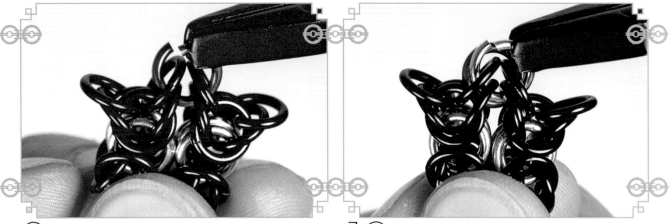

9 With an open brown ring, go through the 4 blue rings following the path of the arrow shown in Step 8. Close the ring. As you add this ring, adjust your arm position as necessary to guide the ring in smoothly (see Don't Be Afraid to Do the Chicken Dance on page 29).

10 Go through the same 4 rings with an aluminum ring, and close the ring.

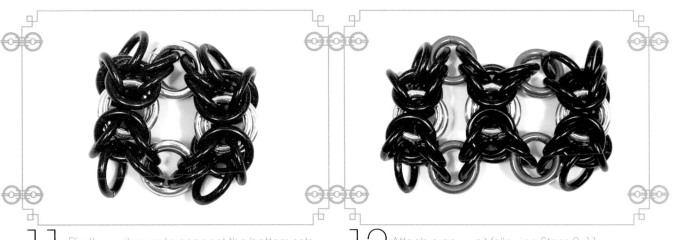

11 Flip the units over to connect the bottom sets of blue rings with a new brown ring and close. Double with an aluminum ring and close.

Here's what your piece should look like at this point. Make sure all aluminum rings are on the same side, and the brown rings are on the reverse side.

12 Attach a new unit following Steps 9–11. Continue in this manner until your piece is the length you desire.

13 When you reach the last unit, add another set of brown and aluminum rings, but do not add a new unit.

14 Go through the aluminum and brown rings at the end of the weave with a new aluminum ring and close.

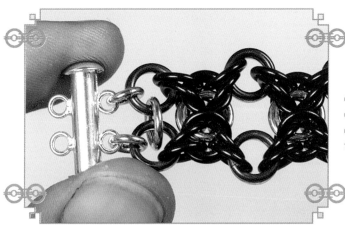

15 Use the tiny clasp rings to attach your clasp to the aluminum and brown rings at the end of the weave. Repeat on the opposite end, and you're done! When you attach the second half of the clasp, orient it so that the clasp will close properly (the small tunnel should slide inside the larger tunnel).

WEAVE IN A NUTSHELL

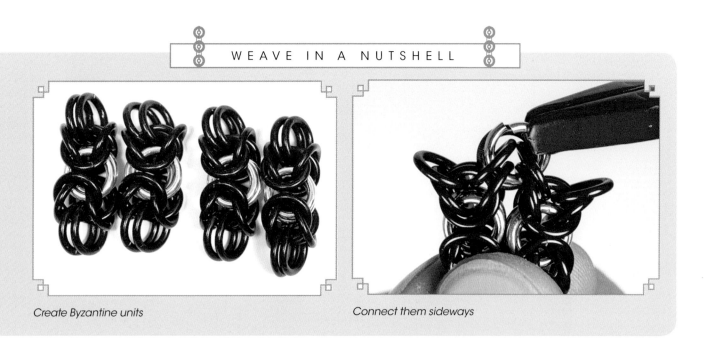

Create Byzantine units

Connect them sideways

*For an elegant, polished Olivia Bracelet,
try sterling silver rings. Precious metal
sizes for this project are listed on page 80.*

Olivia Bracelet Variations

Mini Olivia Bracelet, Dense Olivia Bracelet and Mini Dense Olivia Bracelet

 **advanced**  *Long to Epic project*

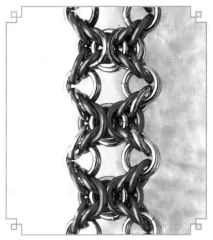  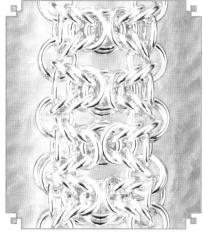

There are a variety of ways you can manipulate this weave for different looks. The simplest is to change ring sizes for a Mini Olivia Bracelet as shown at far left in copper and lime. For this variation, use D20—20 gauge, 1/8" (3.2mm) rings.

Another possible variation is the Dense Olivia Bracelet; this is a variation of Olivia in which your final step is to connect the edging rings (the rings added in Steps 9-11) to one another using new rings, shown here in blue. This pulls the weave in snugly, and completely changes the look. Dense Olivia is possible with a variety of ring sizes, but you may have to play around a bit with the number of Byzantine connector rings—instead of 3, try 2 if your weave is too tight. Additionally, you might need to use smaller rings when you connect the edging rings. Because some troubleshooting might be required, I recommend creating just 3–4 units and connecting

them to make sure your ring sizes work before diving in and creating a zillion units that don't fit together. The Dense Olivia Bracelet shown here uses 2-Connector Byzantine made with anodized aluminum rings in size H18—18 gauge, 3/16" (4.8mm) for the Byzantine portion. The edging rings added to squeeze the Olivia segments closer are size F18 - 18 gauge, 5/32" (4.0 mm).

The final variation shown here at far right is a Mini Dense Olivia Bracelet. This version uses sterling silver E19—19 gauge, 9/64" (3.6mm) throughout.

X-Lock Byzantine Bracelet

 *Intermediate*

MATERIALS LIST FOR A 7¼" (18.4CM) BRACELET

32 thin large jump rings: L18 copper—18 gauge, 1/4" (6.4mm)

8 thick medium jump rings: K16 copper—16 gauge, 15/64" (6.0mm)

53 small jump rings: F18 anodized aluminum—18 gauge, 5/32" (4.0mm)

21 color red

32 color turquoise

4–6 tiny clasp rings: D18 copper—18 gauge, 1/8" (3.2mm)

toggle clasp

TOOLS

2 pairs of flat-nose pliers

piece of wire (optional)

PRECIOUS METAL RING SUBSTITUTIONS

Thin large rings: L17—17 gauge, 1/4" (6.4mm)

Thick medium rings: J14—14 gauge, 7/32" (5.6mm)

Small rings: F17—17 gauge, 5/32" (4.0mm)

This weave is the classic Byzantine weave, but using different ring sizes changes the look completely. Even experienced chain mailers do a double take when they see this pattern. X-Lock uses fewer rings than most bracelets, so it's a great project choice if you're in a hurry, or if you want to splurge on precious metal rings.

These instructions demonstrate a method of speedweaving in which you add "raw" (untouched, straight from the bag) rings and close them as you go, like the Box chain speedweaving variation shown on page 74. Give it a try—you might be surprised at how much time it saves. If using raw rings proves too difficult, then you can pause to pre-close some of the thin, large copper rings and the small turquoise rings. Or, you can eliminate the scooping altogether in Steps 1 and 6, and simply add those rings on one at a time. Your plier grip is different when you open rings using the speedweaving method. The pliers in your non-dominant hand remain further back, even when you open rings. Use the same position as shown on page 29 at left. This way you don't have to set the weave down to open rings (which would defeat the purpose of speedweaving!)

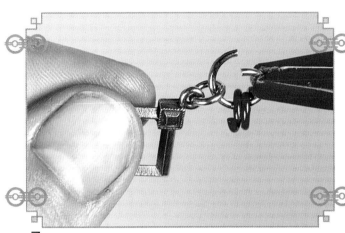

1 Attach a tiny clasp ring to the loop part of the toggle clasp and close the ring (see Closing Jump Rings on pages 20–25). With an open thin large ring, scoop up 2 small turquoise rings and go through the tiny clasp ring (see Learn to Scoop on page 28). Close the large ring.

2 Double the copper ring by adding another thin large ring through the clasp ring and the 2 small turquoise rings. Before moving on, close the 2 turquoise rings.

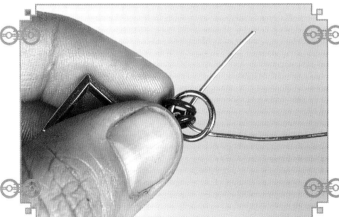

3 Flip the turquoise rings back, just as you did in Steps 4–5 of the *Box Chain Bracelet* on page 71. Because the rings are different sizes, try using a wire to mark the path of the new ring you'll add.

4 Tug on the wire so the rings pop into place.

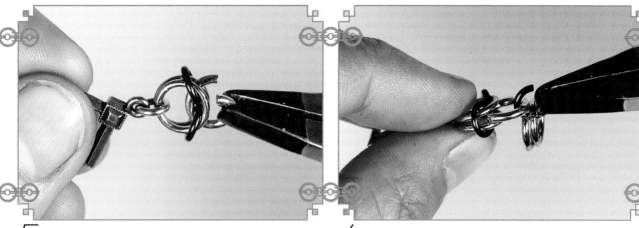

5 Add a thick medium ring to the turquoise rings. See Steps 6–7 of the *Box Chain Bracelet* on page 72 for more information.

6 With a new small turquoise ring, scoop 2 thin large copper rings. Go through the thick medium ring from Step 5. Close the turquoise ring.

7 Add a second turquoise ring through the same 2 thin copper rings and thick medium ring. Close the turquoise ring. Before moving on, close the raw copper rings.

8 Flip back the copper rings. These should flip back more easily than the rings in Steps 3–4, but feel free to use a wire piece if it helps.

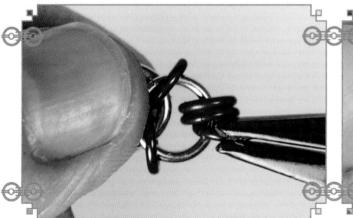

9 Add a small red ring through the flipped-back copper rings. Double, then triple the red ring by adding 2 more red rings through the same 2 copper rings.

10 Now you're back to Step 1. With a new open large copper ring, scoop 2 small turquoise rings, and go through the tripled red rings. Close the copper ring, and then double it with a new copper ring.

11 Repeat Steps 2–10 to create more units.

12 When your bracelet is the length you desire, add a single ring and attach the bar portion of the toggle clasp.

WEAVE IN A NUTSHELL

Add 2 large thin copper rings and 2 turquoise rings. Flip the turquoise rings.

Add a thick medium ring.

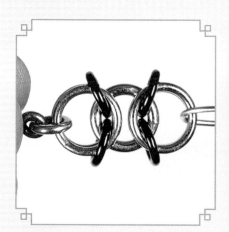

Add 2 more turquoise rings and 2 more large thin copper rings. Flip the copper rings.

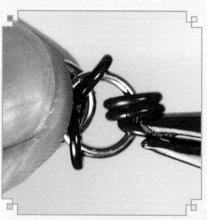

Add 3 red connector rings.

This bracelet looks great in a variety of colors and materials. When I make this bracelet using precious sterling silver (as shown in the bottom bracelet above), I love using niobium or gold-fill rings for the tripled connectors. Use size F18—18 gauge, 5/32" (4.0mm) if you'd like to do the same.

Floating Bead Pendant

advanced

MATERIALS LIST

44 medium jump rings: D19 sterling silver—19 gauge, 1/8" (3.2mm)

12 medium jump rings: D20 anodized niobium, color brown— 20 gauge, 1/8" (3.2mm)

2 slightly larger jump rings: E19 sterling silver—19 gauge, 9/64" (3.6mm)

12 small jump rings: B20 anodized niobium, color brown— 20 gauge, 3/32" (2.4mm)

1 pendant bail

1 bead, 6mm

1 piece of sterling wire or an eyepin

TOOLS

2 pairs of flat-nose pliers

1 pair of round-nose pliers

wire cutters

BASE METAL RING SUBSTITUTIONS

The pendant is much looser in base metal. For extra stability, add doubled rings to the beaded loops in Step 1. You can even triple the rings if your loops are big enough.

Medium rings: D20—20 gauge, 1/8" (3.2 mm) (Note that you combine the D19 [silver] and D20 [anodized] rings into this one size.)

Small rings: B20—20 gauge, 3/32" (2.4 mm)

Slightly-larger rings: E20—20 gauge, 9/64" (3.6 mm)

This elegant, eye-catching pendant combines a Japanese edging with Byzantine; the bead appears to magically float within the chain mail diamond.

The instructions here use the speedweaving method. If you don't want to speedweave, prepare for the weave by opening all D20 rings, all E19 rings, 28 D19 rings and 8 B20 rings. Close 16 D19 rings and 4 B20 rings.

1 Use the Basic Wire Loop technique on pages 30–31 to create loops on each side of your bead. The two loops should be on the same plane, as shown above. Add 2 medium sterling silver rings to one loop and close each ring (see Closing Jump Rings on pages 20–25). These rings are the two connectors that begin your Byzantine unit.

2 With a new medium sterling silver ring, scoop 2 additional sterling silver rings and weave through the 2 rings you added in Step 1 (see Learn to Scoop on page 28). Close the ring.

3 Double that ring with a new medium sterling silver and close. Flip those sterling silver rings back, following Steps 4–5 in the *Box Chain Bracelet* on page 71. Add 3 medium anodized niobium connector rings.

4 With a new sterling silver medium ring, scoop 2 additional sterling silver rings. Weave through the 3 connector rings and close. Double the sterling ring.

5 Flip the sterling rings back, and add a new medium sterling silver ring. Before closing, add 2 of the small niobium rings. Double the sterling silver ring as you would any other connector ring, being sure to also pass through the 2 niobium rings.

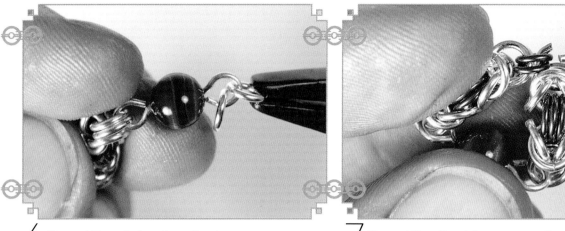

6 Repeat Steps 1–4 on the other loop.

7 Repeat Step 5, adding your medium connector as usual, but instead of adding new niobium rings, weave the new ring through the 2 niobium rings you added in Step 5. Be sure the weave is not twisted, and both sets of tripled niobium connectors are facing outward.

8 Now you'll repeat the weave on the opposite side of the bead; with a medium sterling silver ring, scoop 2 other sterling silver rings and weave through the 2 connectors from Step 1. Repeat Steps 3–7 for the other side of the weave.

9 Add 1 small niobium ring onto 1 of the connector sets at the end of the weave.

10 Add 3 more small niobium rings so that 2 hang from each of the 2-connector sets at the end of the weave.

11 With a slightly larger sterling silver ring, weave through the 4 hanging niobium rings and close.

12 Repeat Steps 9–11 on the other side of the weave, being sure to attach the pendant bail before closing the ring. If your bail faces a different direction than the one used in the tutorial you will need a tiny sterling silver ring to connect the weave to the bail. Your pendant won't be stiff, but it will hold its shape well enough to lie flat when worn.

Floating Bead Necklace

For a truly special variation on this weave, create several of the floating bead units, along with beads trapped in jump rings (following the Trapping the Bead technique on page 43) and connect them together to form a show-stopping necklace.

Change ring color, bead color or both for a unique look!

93

Helm

Our journey continues with the classic Helm weave and additional patterns that build from a Helm base. The origins of the Helm weave are elusive, though it is widely accepted to be an ancient Scandinavian design.

The structure of this weave would categorize it as belonging to the Japanese family—notice the horizontal and vertical connections. However, a new element of "captive rings" has been introduced. Captive rings are rings that are trapped in place—or "sandwiched in," as I am fond of saying—by adjacent rings. The captive rings themselves do not link through any other rings. You may also hear the captive ring referred to as an orbital ring, since it "orbits" around smaller rings without actually linking through them.

After you learn Helm chain (also known as Parallel chain), you can move to any of the variations in this chapter, and build upon techniques learned from previous chapters. Combine Helm chain with a Japanese edging to create the *Lancelot Bracelet* on page 116, or connect Helm to 3-Connector Byzantine for the spectacular *Rondo à la Byzantine Necklace* on page 104, or its companion bracelet on page 110. A special thanks is due to Carol Branting (known as PrairieGal online), whose Rondo and Camelot weaves inspired me to create Rondo à la Byzantine and Lancelot.

Many of the main projects in this chapter are sterling silver. You've seen colorful projects in the first two project chapters, and more will come in the next Coiled chapter. In this chapter I wanted to pay homage to the structure of chain mail, without the distraction of colors and beads. The simple lines of Helm chain are elegant and sophisticated exactly as they are. The ring intersections of Rondo à la Byzantine are aesthetic and intricate even in one color.

By now you know that I love working with colored rings. But for some reason, to me, these weaves are striking in sterling silver. Of course, this is not to say that you, too, are required to have similar preferences. Feel free to customize your piece as you wish. The step-by-step photos always use rings of contrasting colors, not just for clarity, but also to inspire you to discover the various ways colored rings can enhance certain aspects of each weave to your liking. Think of these projects as blank canvases—add whatever embellishments you wish!

Helm Chain Necklace

Long project

MATERIALS LIST FOR AN 18" (45.7CM) NECKLACE

85 large jump rings: S14 sterling silver—14 gauge, 23/64" (9.1mm)

62 medium jump rings: K15 sterling silver—15 gauge, 15/64" (6.0mm) (shown in purple in the step-by-step photos)

5 small clasp rings: F16 sterling silver—16 gauge, 5/32" (4.0mm)

clasp

TOOLS

2 pairs of flat-nose pliers

2 pairs of duckbill pliers to close the large rings (optional)

BASE METAL RING SUBSTITUTIONS

Large rings: T16—16 gauge, 3/8" (9.5mm)

Medium rings: L16—16 gauge, 1/4" (6.4mm)

This versatile pattern is easy to dress up or down and is perfect for a variety of style preferences. As you'll discover in subsequent projects, Helm chain is an ideal starting point for expanding into increasingly complicated designs.

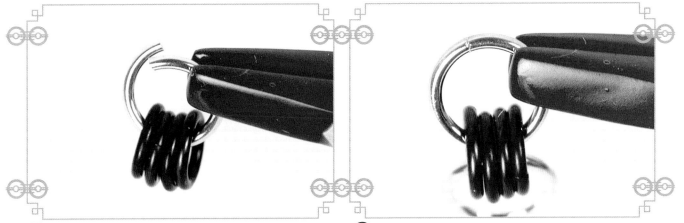

1 Before weaving, close the medium jump rings (shown here in purple) and open the large rings (see Closing Jump Rings on pages 20–25 and Opening Jump Rings on pages 26–27). Scoop 4 medium rings onto 1 large ring; close the large ring (see Learn to Scoop on page 28).

2 Double the large ring by going through the same 4 medium rings. Close this large ring.

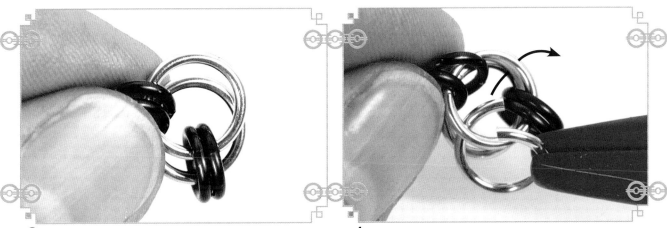

3 Bring the large rings together so they are stacked. Separate the group of 4 medium rings into 2 groups of 2 rings.

4 Weave a new large ring in between the 2 large rings and close. This ring surrounds 2 of the medium rings, but it does not go through them.

5 Repeat Step 4 on the other side of the unit, surrounding the other 2 medium rings.

6 Your weave should look like the picture above from the side. The two large rings "sandwich in" the single large ring you just added on each side.

7   Scoop 2 medium rings with an open large ring, and go through the previous 2 medium rings. Close the large ring.

8   Flip the piece over. Your next ring will follow the same path as the large ring added in Step 7 through the 4 medium rings, but on the other side of the weave.

9   With an open large ring, first go through the 2 medium rings that are held tight in the weave, then slide the ring through the 2 medium hanging rings. Close the large ring.

10   With a new large open ring, weave in between the previous pair of large rings, just like you did in Step 4. Close the ring.

11   Repeat Steps 7–10 until your piece is the length you desire, minus the length that will be added by the clasp (usually 1" or 2.5cm).

12   Finish with a set of small rings, instead of large rings, one on each side of the weave, "sandwiching in" the last large ring.

 13 Attach half of the clasp to the small rings at each end of the necklace. Use small rings to form a short chain to attach the bar portion of the clasp to the necklace.

Add your choice of embellishments for a personalized project. Try color, change ring sizes, or shorten the length of the weave to create a bracelet. Use your imagination!

 WEAVE IN A NUTSHELL

Add a large "sandwich" ring.

Scoop 2 medium rings with a large ring and weave through the previous medium rings.

Weave a new large ring through the 4 medium rings. Repeat!

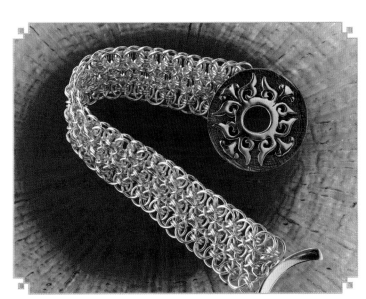

Multi-Strand Variation

Try using tiny rings for a delicate, intricate version. This bracelet shows multiple strands of Helm chain connected to make a cuff. For a mini Helm like this, use sizes I20—20 gauge, 13/64" (5.2mm) and D20—20 gauge, 1/8" (3.2mm) in base metal or sizes I19—19 gauge, 13/64" (5.2mm) and D20—20 gauge, 1/8" (3.2mm) in sterling silver, gold-fill or niobium.

Helm Wave Bracelet

advanced  *Mid-length project*

MATERIALS LIST FOR A 7¾" (19.7CM) BRACELET

FOR HELM CHAIN

16 large jump rings: N18 bronze—18 gauge, 9/32" (7.1mm)

49 slightly larger jump rings: O18 stainless steel—18 gauge, 19/64" (7.5mm)

42 medium jump rings: H18 stainless steel—18 gauge, 3/16" (4.8mm)

FOR WAVE

14 extra large jump rings: P18 bronze—18 gauge, 5/16" (7.9mm)

28 medium jump rings: G18 bronze—18 gauge, 11/64" (4.4mm)

14 small jump rings: E18 bronze—18 gauge, 9/64" (3.6mm)

2–6 tiny clasp rings: D18 bronze—18 gauge, 1/8" (3.2mm)

clasp

TOOLS

2 pairs of flat-nose pliers

PRECIOUS METAL RING SUBSTITUTIONS

For Helm Chain

Large rings: N16—16 gauge, 9/32" (7.1mm)

Slightly larger rings: O16—16 gauge, 19/64" (7.5mm)

Medium rings: H17—17 gauge, 3/16" (4.8mm)

For Wave

Extra large rings: P16—16 gauge, 5/16" (7.9mm)

Medium rings: G17—17 gauge, 11/64" (4.4mm)

Small rings: F17—17 gauge, 5/32" (4.0mm)

This slinky variation of Helm chain is one of my favorite patterns. It's simple enough to make in an afternoon, and unusual enough to draw compliments whenever I wear it. This project has an advanced rating because stainless steel and bronze are difficult to work with. However, the result is a bracelet that will last for hundreds—if not thousands!—of years. If the metals are too tough for you, feel free to substitute copper and aluminum for an easier, intermediate-level project.

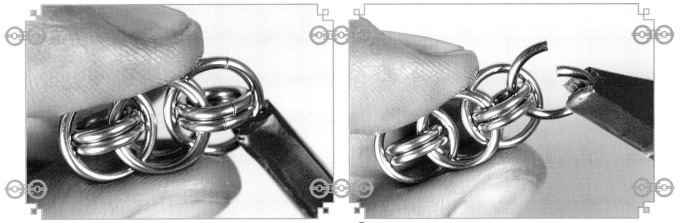

1 To prepare, close the medium stainless steel jump rings and open the remaining rings (see Closing Jump Rings on pages 20–25 and Opening Jump Rings on pages 26–27). If you are an advanced weaver, try closing the medium and small bronze rings and scooping them into the weave as the Helm chain is made. Refer to Steps 4-5 to see the pattern of the bronze hanging rings.

Steps 1–3 use the Helm Chain rings only. Set aside the Wave rings so you don't get confused.

Using the large and medium stainless steel rings, follow Steps 1–5 of the *Helm Chain Necklace* on page 97 to get the weave started.

2 Add 2 large bronze rings to mark the end of the first section of the weave, 1 on each side of the weave, "sandwiching in" the last large ring.

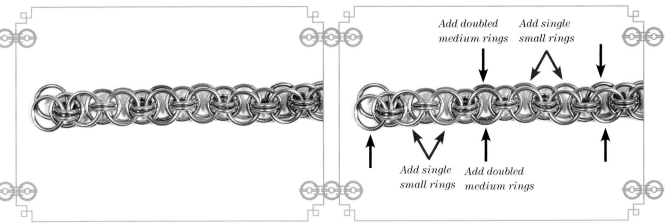

Add doubled
medium rings

Add single
small rings

Add single
small rings

Add doubled
medium rings

3 Continue to weave the Helm chain, making sure that every third set of doubled rings is bronze instead of stainless steel. Your weave needs to end with one of these bronze sets. You need to make your base chain quite long because it will shrink about 40 percent when you add the Wave.

4 To begin the Wave, add medium and small bronze rings to every set of doubled rings. Onto the bronze doubled rings, add 4 medium bronze rings (2 on each side of the weave). Add 1 small ring to each set of doubled stainless steel rings.

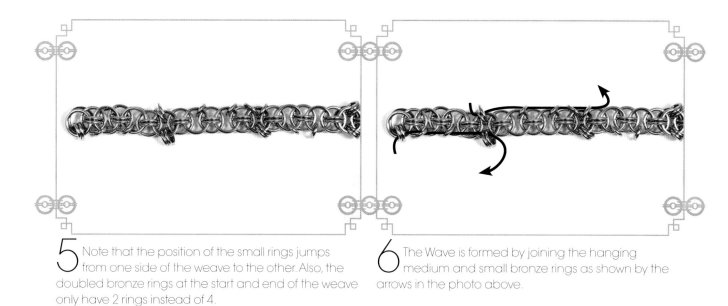

5 Note that the position of the small rings jumps from one side of the weave to the other. Also, the doubled bronze rings at the start and end of the weave only have 2 rings instead of 4.

6 The Wave is formed by joining the hanging medium and small bronze rings as shown by the arrows in the photo above.

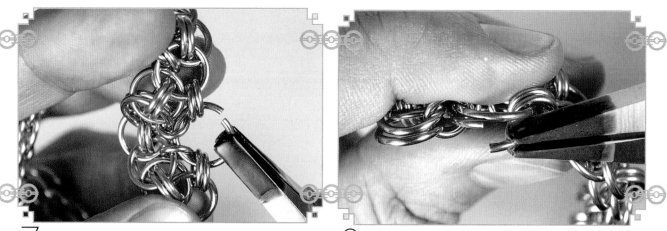

7 With an open extra large bronze ring, weave through the first 6 hanging rings at the beginning of the weave. You'll pass through a doubled set of medium bronze rings, then 2 single small bronze rings, and finally through another doubled set of medium bronze rings. Close the extra large ring.

8 Double the extra large bronze ring by passing a new ring through the same 6 hanging rings. Do not open this ring too wide, or it will be difficult to add without crossing it through the first extra large bronze ring.

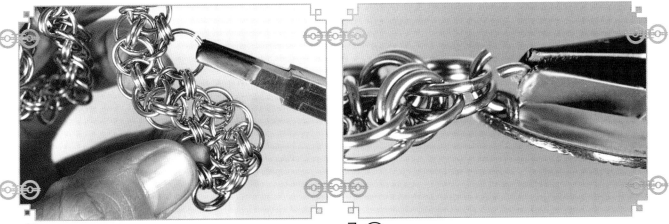

9 With a new extra large bronze ring, weave through the next 6 hanging rings. They are on the opposite end of the weave, so you should flip the weave over for better access. Double this ring, and continue the Wave pattern to the end of the bracelet.

10 Attach the clasp to the bronze rings at the beginning and end of the bracelet.

Tip

As long as your Helm chain strand is flexible and supple, you can use a range of ring sizes to create the Wave. You might need to do some trial and error to find a combination that works well, but there are definitely numerous possibilities. If the Helm chain doesn't lie flat when you start to create the Wave, then the problem likely is with the Helm chain. Try increasing the inner diameter size of the large rings, or even decreasing the wire diameter size of the small rings.

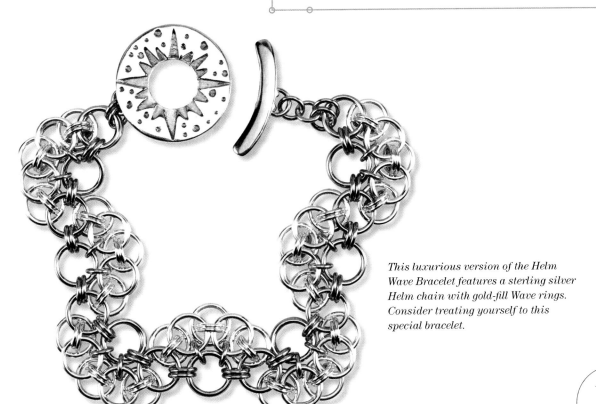

This luxurious version of the Helm Wave Bracelet features a sterling silver Helm chain with gold-fill Wave rings. Consider treating yourself to this special bracelet.

Rondo à la Byzantine Necklace

advanced

Epic project

MATERIALS LIST FOR AN 18" (45.7CM) NECKLACE

107 large jump rings: N16 sterling silver—16 gauge, 9/32" (7.1mm)

548 medium jump rings: H17 sterling silver—17 gauge, 3/16" (4.8mm)

2 small clasp rings: F16 sterling silver—16 gauge, 5/32" (4.0mm)

3–5 tiny clasp rings: D17 sterling silver—17 gauge, 1/8" (3.2mm)

clasp

TOOLS

2 pairs of flat-nose pliers

BASE METAL RING SUBSTITUTIONS

Large rings: N18—18 gauge, 9/32" (7.1mm)

Medium rings: H18—18 gauge, 3/16" (4.8mm)

This necklace combines Helm chain with Byzantine for an intricate collar reminiscent of Egyptian royalty. With more than 650 rings, this weighty necklace is not for the faint of heart. Expect heads to turn and be prepared for many oohs and ahhs whenever you wear this piece.

Instructions for opening and closing rings are not included in this project because each student will have their own preferences of using pre-opened or pre-closed rings; Step 5 recommends using raw rings straight from the package, with no preparation required. After reading through each step, you may wish to pre-open or pre-close a small amount of rings, depending on your weaving preferences.

1 Follow Steps 1–11 of the *Helm Chain Necklace* on pages 97–98 to create the starting point for the necklace. Work until the Helm chain is the length you desire for your necklace minus 1" (2.5cm) for the clasp.

2 Begin to create Byzantine: Add a pair of medium rings to each of the large doubled rings. Add a pair of medium rings to each pair of the medium rings that were just added. (Even though the bottom rings look single from this perspective, they are indeed doubled.)

3 Go to the beginning of the weave and flip the bottom set of doubled medium rings back as instructed in Steps 4–5 of the *Box Chain Bracelet* on page 71. Add a medium connector ring.

4 Add 2 more connector rings for a total of 3 connector rings, and then do the same for each set of doubled hanging rings.

5 Go back to the beginning of the weave. With a new medium ring, scoop up 2 raw medium rings, weave the medium ring through the connector rings and close. Do not open or close the raw rings, simply leave them as is for now.

6 Double the medium ring from Step 5 and close. Add linked pairs of doubled rings in the same manner to the remainder of the weave, being sure to leave the bottom set raw.

7 Go back to the beginning, to the first 2 Box weave rings that are angled in toward one another. The first example of these rings is highlighted in blue above.

8 With a new open medium ring, weave through the 2 Box weave rings following the path of the arrow from Step 7 and close.

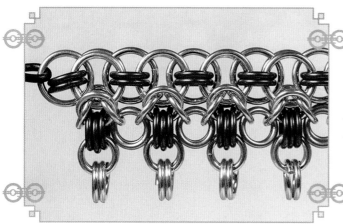

9 Double this ring with a new medium ring. I call these rings "doubled side connectors" because they connect the Byzantine units to one another, and they are doubled. Repeat Steps 8–9 for the entire weave.

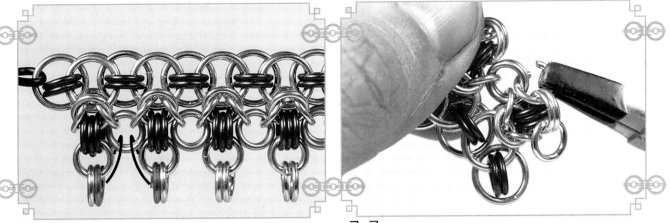

10 In this last stage of the weave, you'll flip the raw rings back (the first set is shown here in blue), and attach them to the doubled side connectors.

11 Close the hanging raw medium ring at the very beginning without attaching it to anything. Go to the other raw hanging ring on that first set, open it, weave it through the first set of doubled side connectors, and close.

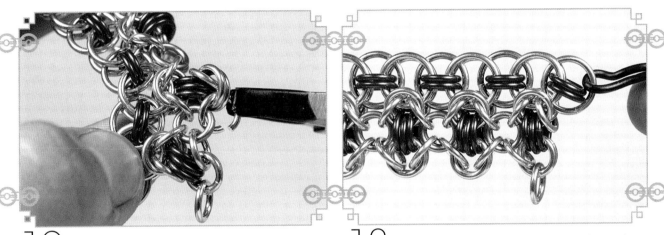

12 Move to the next set of raw hanging rings. Open the one closest to the beginning of the weave, and thread it back through the first set of doubled side connectors. You may find it easier to open the left side of the ring toward you, and weave it in "backward" as shown in the photo. Close the ring.

13 Continue opening the raw rings and weaving them through their adjacent doubled side connectors. Your very last hanging ring simply gets closed without going through any other rings, just like the first ring you closed in Step 11.

14 Pull up the hanging ring at the end of the weave and attach a set of doubled side connectors through the 2 free Box rings.

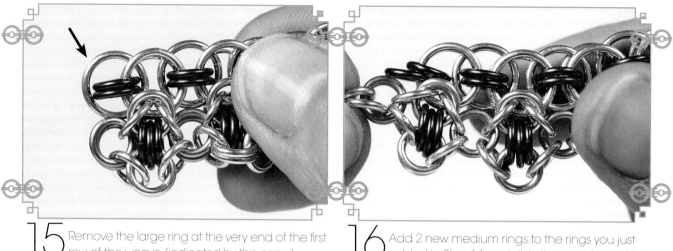

15
Remove the large ring at the very end of the first row of the weave (indicated by the arrow).

16
Add 2 new medium rings to the rings you just added in Step 14 and slide them up toward the medium rings in the Helm row above.

17
Weave a clasp ring through the 4 medium rings at the end of the weave; the 2 you just added, plus the 2 Helm chain rings.

18
Attach your clasp to this medium ring, or, depending on the orientation of the clasp, close this ring and use another ring to attach the clasp. (The photo above shows the clasp being attached to the sterling silver version of the necklace.)

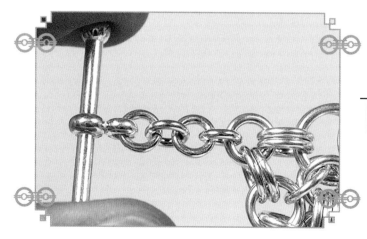

19
Repeat Steps 15-18 to attach the opposite end of the clasp.

The photo on page 115 shows these steps, plus and additional step that adds Helm chain to the opposite side of the weave.

1. *Create the Helm chain*
2. *Add 2 sets of 2 hanging rings*
3. *Flip and add 3 connectors for Byzantine*
4. *Add 2 sets of 2 hanging rings—leave the bottom ones raw*
5. *Add the center connectors; flip and connect the raw hanging rings*

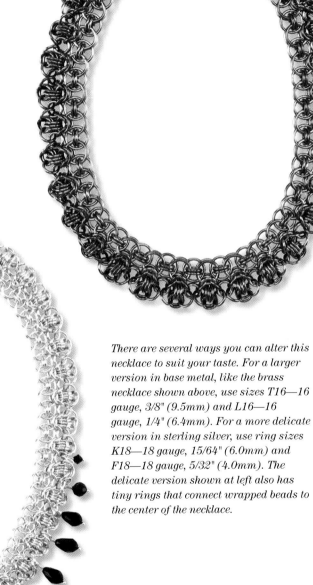

There are several ways you can alter this necklace to suit your taste. For a larger version in base metal, like the brass necklace shown above, use sizes T16—16 gauge, 3/8" (9.5mm) and L16—16 gauge, 1/4" (6.4mm). For a more delicate version in sterling silver, use ring sizes K18—18 gauge, 15/64" (6.0mm) and F18—18 gauge, 5/32" (4.0mm). The delicate version shown at left also has tiny rings that connect wrapped beads to the center of the necklace.

Rondo à la Byzantine Bracelet

expert

Long project

MATERIALS LIST FOR A 7 ¼" (18.4CM) BRACELET

104 large jump rings: K18 sterling silver—18 gauge, 15/64" (6.0mm)

291 medium jump rings: F18 sterling silver—18 gauge, 5/32" (4.0mm)

FOR THE CLASP

4 large rings: H18 sterling sliver—18 gauge, 3/16" (4.8mm)

12 medium rings: F18 sterling—18 gauge, 5/32" (4.0mm)

6–12 tiny rings: D17 sterling silver—17 gauge, 1/8" (3.2mm)

3-strand slide clasp

TOOLS

2 pairs of flat-nose pliers

wire piece (optional)

BASE METAL RING SUBSTITUTIONS

The following sizes were used in the step-by-step photos. They create a slightly larger piece than the sterling silver version.

Large rings: N18—18 gauge, 9/32" (7.1mm)

Medium rings: H18—18 gauge, 3/16" (4.8mm)

This weave takes chain mail to a new level. You'll treasure this hefty bracelet for years to come. With approximately 60 rings per inch for the sterling silver version (slightly less for base metal), this dense weave requires patience and persistence, but the result is absolutely worth it!

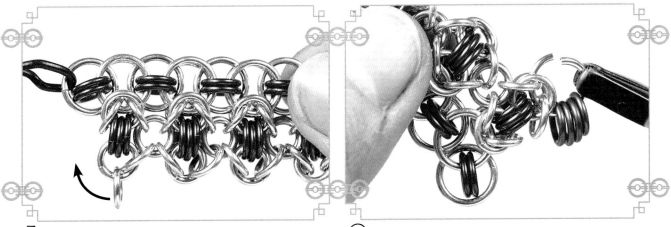

1 Follow Steps 1–14 of *Rondo à la Byzantine Necklace* on pages 105–107, with the exception that this piece should be bracelet length. Make your bracelet the desired length, minus ½" (1.3cm) for the clasp.

Open the remaining large rings. Close at least 4 of the remaining medium rings. Depending on your skill level, you may be able to close all the medium rings and still execute later steps with ease. If you have difficulty adding the closed rings at Step 6, simply open them and add them one at a time after Step 8.

Flip the first hanging ring back to create a Box unit.

2 With a new large ring, scoop 4 closed medium rings and weave the large ring through the Box unit at the end of the weave. Close the large ring.

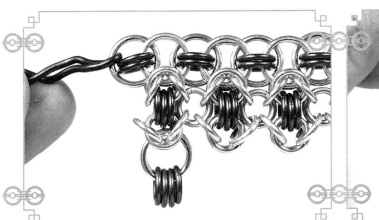

3 With a new large ring, double the ring you just added. The ring goes through the Box unit as well as the 4 medium rings.

4 Add a new large ring sandwiched in between the large rings you added in Step 3. This large ring encircles 2 of the medium rings (just like Step 4 of the *Helm Chain Necklace* on page 97). Close the large ring.

As you continue, concentrate on weaving Helm chain exactly as you did for the first row of this weave. The only difference is that the doubled rings will also be going through Box units of the row above. Try not to be distracted by this difference!

5 With a new open large ring, scoop 2 closed medium rings and go through the next Box unit. Before closing the large ring, also pass it through the previous 2 medium rings that you encircled in Step 4.

6 Close the large ring. Verify that it goes through the Box unit, plus 4 medium rings. (If you couldn't add the medium rings in Step 5, it's OK. Keep them off for now, and add them after Step 8.)

7 Flip the weave over to find the path of your new large ring. It goes through the 4 medium rings (just like Step 9 of the *Helm Chain Necklace* on page 98), and also passes through the same Box unit from Steps 5–6.

8 Weave the new large ring through and close it. (If you didn't scoop the 2 medium rings in Step 5, add them now, so that your piece matches the photo for Step 9.)

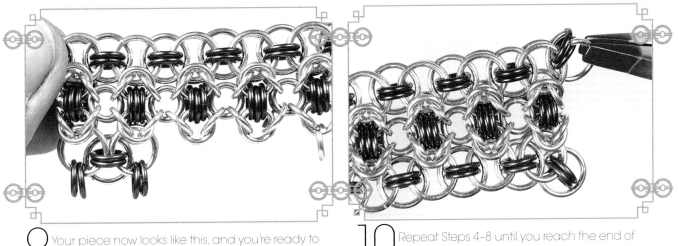

9 Your piece now looks like this, and you're ready to add a new "sandwiched" Helm chain ring, just like in Step 4.

10 Repeat Steps 4–8 until you reach the end of the weave. You'll end with a sandwiched ring.

11 Exactly as in Step 12 of the Helm Chain Necklace on page 98, add 2 medium rings at the end of the Helm strands.

12 Add a large clasp ring (this ring size is slightly smaller than the "large" rings used in the Helm chain) through the side of the last Byzantine unit and close the ring.

13 Double the ring you just added.

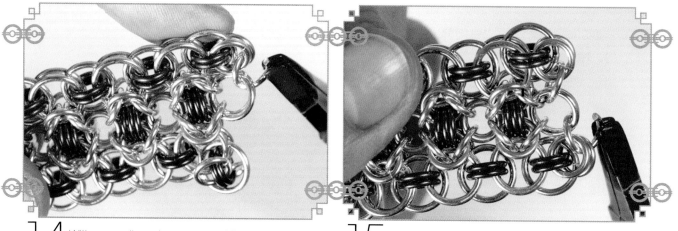

14 With a medium ring, connect the doubled rings you just added to the end of one Helm chain strand.

15 Repeat Step 14 for the second Helm chain strand.

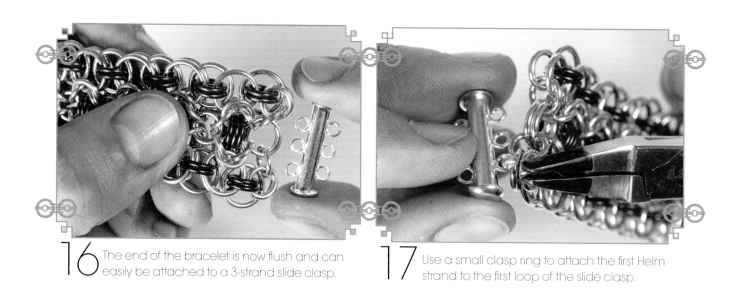

16 The end of the bracelet is now flush and can easily be attached to a 3-strand slide clasp.

17 Use a small clasp ring to attach the first Helm strand to the first loop of the slide clasp.

18 Repeat Step 17 for the center rings and the second Helm strand. Flip the weave over and repeat Steps 11-18 to complete your piece. If the loops in your clasp allow, you may double all the clasp rings for added strength.

WEAVE IN A NUTSHELL

1. Create the Helm chain
2. Add 2 sets of 2 hanging rings
3. Flip and add 3 connectors for Byzantine
4. Add 2 sets of 2 hanging rings—leave the bottom ones raw
5. Add the center connectors; flip and connect the raw hanging rings
6. Finish the Helm chain

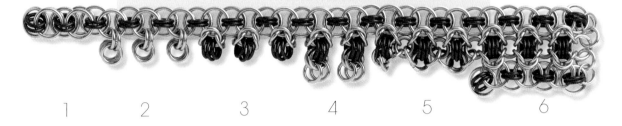

1   2   3   4   5   6

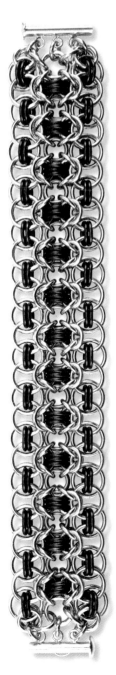

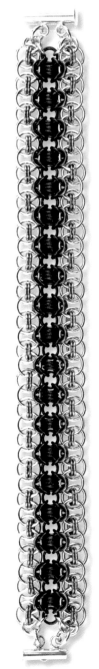

To duplicate the color pattern used in the step-by-step photos, use the following rings in the colors noted here, or substitute colors of your choosing:
86 N18 aluminum rings for Helm chain
60 H18 brown rings for Helm chain
112 H18 aluminum rings for the Box units
42 H18 brown rings for the 3-connector Byzantine
26 H18 yellow rings for the doubled side connectors
12 H18 aluminum rings at the clasp
4 K18 aluminum rings for Steps 12–13.
For a tiny version of this weave, as shown in the bracelet in the photo at right, use these base metal sizes:
I20—20 gauge, 13/64" (5.2mm)
D20—20 gauge, 1/8" (3.2mm)
Or these precious metal sizes:
I19—19 gauge, 13/64" (5.2mm)
D20—20 gauge, 1/8" (3.2mm)

Lancelot Bracelet

advanced

MATERIALS LIST FOR A 7¾" (19.7CM) BRACELET

HELM CHAIN AND CLASP

50 large jump rings: N16 sterling—16 gauge, 9/32" (7.1mm)

19 medium jump rings: H17 sterling—17 gauge, 3/16" (4.8mm)

3–6 small clasp rings: D17 sterling—17 gauge, 1/8" (3.2mm)

clasp

LANCELOT EDGING

28 medium jump rings : H17 sterling—17 gauge, 3/16" (4.8mm)

112 small jump rings: F17 sterling—17 gauge, 5/32" (4.0mm) (shown in purple)

56 thin tiny rings: D20 sterling—20 gauge, 1/8" (3.2mm)

28 thick tiny rings: D17 sterling—17 gauge, 1/8" (3.2mm)

TOOLS

2 pairs of flat-nose pliers

wire piece (optional)

BASE METAL RING SUBSTITUTIONS

See page 119

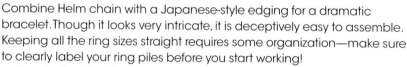

Combine Helm chain with a Japanese-style edging for a dramatic bracelet. Though it looks very intricate, it is deceptively easy to assemble. Keeping all the ring sizes straight requires some organization—make sure to clearly label your ring piles before you start working!

The sterling silver bracelet shown has seven diamond shapes, and makes a bracelet nearly 8" (20.3cm) long. If you remove one diamond, the bracelet is less than 7" (17.8cm), which is too small for most folks. As a happy medium, you can use one less diamond, and then extend the Helm base one unit before attaching the clasp; the bracelet on page 119 uses this lengthening method.

Tip

If you are doing a color version, note the placement of the violet rings—each medium ring alternates color, beginning with a non-colored ring, and ending with a non-colored ring at the end of the weave. This bracelet creates 7 "diamond" shapes, so you'll need 7 violet rings, 1 for the center of each diamond.

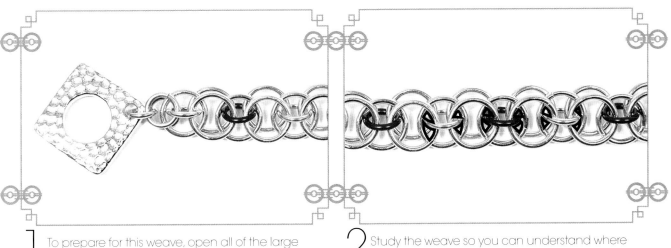

1 To prepare for this weave, open all of the large Helm chain jump rings and 4 of the medium Helm chain jump rings; close the remaining medium Helm chain rings (see Closing Jump Rings on pages 20–25 and Opening Jump Rings on pages 26–27). Open all of the Lancelot edging rings.

Create a strand of Helm chain (Steps 1-12 of the *Helm Chain Necklace* on pages 97–98); however, instead of adding pairs of medium rings, only add single rings. Be sure to finish the ends of your strand exactly like the *Helm Chain Necklace* by adding a set of doubled small rings leading to the clasp (Step 12 of the *Helm Chain Necklace*).

2 Study the weave so you can understand where you'll add the edging rings. Each edging ring will be adjacent to a medium connector from Step 1, and it will go through the "eyes" indicated in the photo above. Each ring you add goes through 3 large rings—a set of doubled rings and a single "sandwiched" center ring. You might need to open your rings slightly wider than normal in order to fit through; you can also try threading a wire piece through first to mark the path of the ring.

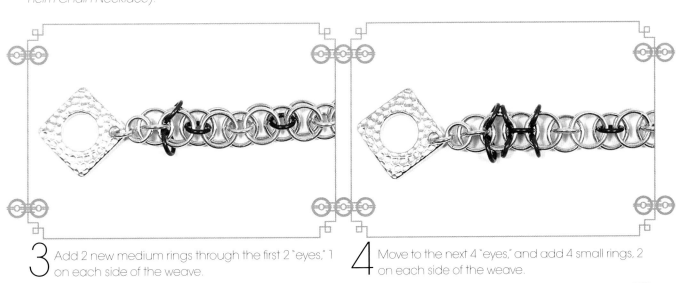

3 Add 2 new medium rings through the first 2 "eyes," 1 on each side of the weave.

4 Move to the next 4 "eyes," and add 4 small rings, 2 on each side of the weave.

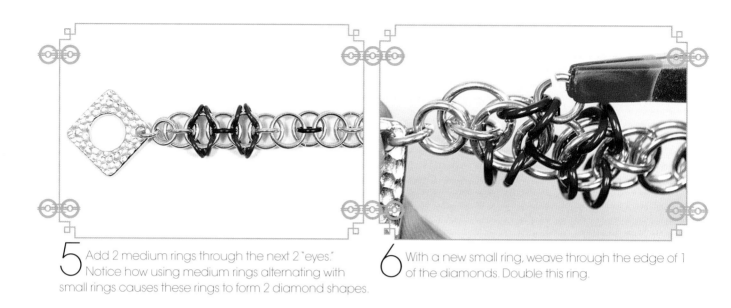

5 Add 2 medium rings through the next 2 "eyes." Notice how using medium rings alternating with small rings causes these rings to form 2 diamond shapes.

6 With a new small ring, weave through the edge of 1 of the diamonds. Double this ring.

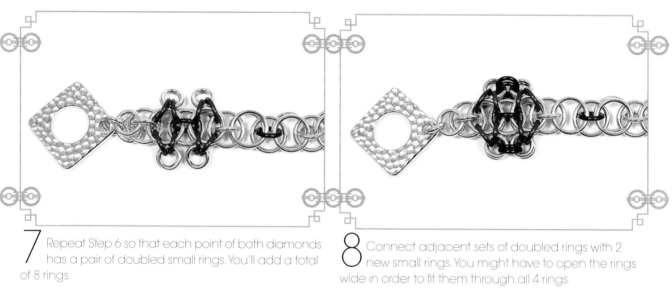

7 Repeat Step 6 so that each point of both diamonds has a pair of doubled small rings. You'll add a total of 8 rings.

8 Connect adjacent sets of doubled rings with 2 new small rings. You might have to open the rings wide in order to fit them through all 4 rings.

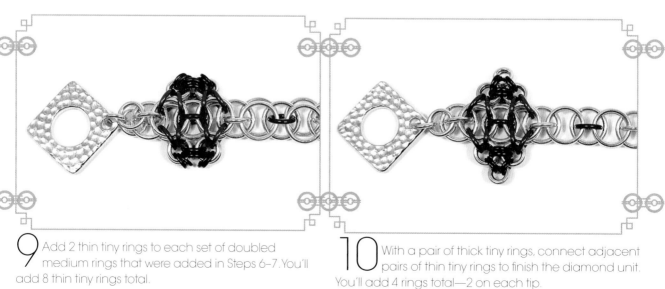

9 Add 2 thin tiny rings to each set of doubled medium rings that were added in Steps 6–7. You'll add 8 thin tiny rings total.

10 With a pair of thick tiny rings, connect adjacent pairs of thin tiny rings to finish the diamond unit. You'll add 4 rings total—2 on each tip.
Repeat Steps 3–10 for the rest of the weave.

BASE METAL RING SUBSTITUTIONS

To duplicate the color pattern used in the step-by-step photos, use the following rings in the colors noted here, or in the colors of your choice. Remember, if you make a shorter bracelet (as shown in the sample above), you'll use fewer of each ring.

Helm Chain and Clasp

50 large jump rings: N18 aluminum—18 gauge, 9/32" (7.1mm)

19 medium jump rings: H18 aluminum and anodized aluminum—18 gauge, 3/16" (4.8mm)

7 color violet

12 non-colored

3–6 small clasp rings: D18 aluminum—18 gauge, 1/8" (3.2mm)

Lancelot Edging

28 medium jump rings: H18 anodized aluminum, color blue—18 gauge, 3/16" (4.8mm)

112 small jump rings: F18 aluminum and anodized aluminum—18 gauge 5/32" (4.0mm)

28 color blue

28 color purple

56 non-colored

56 thin tiny jump rings: D20 anodized aluminum, color purple—20 gauge, 1/8" (3.2mm)

28 thick tiny rings: D18 aluminum—18 gauge, 1/8" (3.2mm)

Lancelot Bracelet Variations

Half Lancelot
Stop after Step 8 and repeat that motif all the way through. This creates a bracelet that looks more like joined hexagons than joined diamonds.

Lancelot Zigzag
Create an offset version of Lancelot by staggering the edging. Complete Steps 1-10 for one side of the weave. When beginning to repeat those steps on the opposite side, skip the first 2 "eyes" and start with the third "eye." Whenever possible, I prefer to adjust the length of the bracelet smaller or larger so that one end starts on the up side, and the other end finishes on the down side.

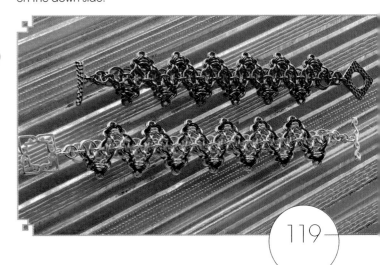

Coiled

Our chain mail journey concludes with the intricate technique of coiling. I use this term because the formation of jump rings in these weaves looks like small coils of wire, rather than individual jump rings. Many weaves can be coiled, but I find the ones in the Japanese family work best, due to their perfectly horizontal rings, which are easily coiled.

I started coiling with earrings, but I later adapted the technique into a finger ring pattern, the *Coiled Ring* on page 126. Those rings quickly became best sellers, and they continue to draw attention at jewelry shows to this day. Still, it was several more years before I realized the full potential of coiling.

I'll never know what possessed me to look at a Japanese 12-in-2 bracelet and contemplate what it would look like with an absurd number of rings crammed into every edge. Somehow, inspiration struck, and the result, the *Coiled Japanese Lace Bracelet* on page 134, was even more impressive than what I'd imagined. Once the Japanese sample was created, the floodgates opened, and I wanted to coil everything I could. I love how adding a coiled border gives the base weave an entirely new look. The edging turns fuzzy, almost like a soft and furry shag carpet.

This technique is ridiculously easy to understand, but incredibly time-consuming to execute. If you're in a hurry, the coiled bracelet weaves are not for you, with the exception of the *Coiled X-Lock Byzantine Bracelet* on page 128. However, if you're willing to devote the time, you'll create a masterpiece of chain mail the likes of which few have seen.

So roll up your sleeves, stretch your fingers and prepare to open and close lots and lots of rings. As always, don't limit yourself to coiling what you see in this book. The next few pages are just the tip of the iceberg in terms of what's possible with this technique. Onward, ho!

Basic Coiled Choker

MATERIALS LIST FOR AN 18" (45.7CM) NECKLACE

56 extra large jump rings: T16 jewelry brass—16 gauge, 3/8" (9.5mm)

497 medium jump rings: H19 enameled copper, color eggplant— 19 gauge, 3/16" (4.8mm)

4 small jump rings: F18 jewelry brass—18 gauge, 5/32" (4.0mm)

toggle clasp

TOOLS

2 pairs of flat-nose pliers

2 pairs of duckbill pliers to close the large rings (optional)

PRECIOUS METAL RING SUBSTITUTIONS

Extra large rings: T14—14 gauge, 3/8" (9.5mm)

Medium rings: You can use the same size enameled copper rings as those listed above, or you can use anodized niobium: H18—18 gauge, 3/16" (4.8mm).

To make a longer choker, add 3–4 extra large rings and 30 medium jump rings per extra inch of length.

Colored rings ebb and flow in gentle waves around your neck in this dramatic choker. It's a basic pattern, but the large number of rings required means you'll likely need more than an afternoon to complete this project.

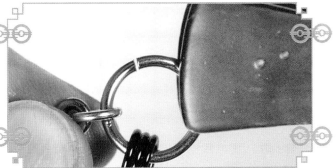

1 Open all of the brass rings, and close all of the enameled copper rings (see Closing Jump Rings on pages 20–25 and Opening Jump Rings on pages 26–27). (Or, you can leave the enameled copper rings raw and close them as you go.) Weave a small jewelry brass ring through the toggle and close.

2 With a large brass ring, scoop 3 enameled copper rings and weave the large ring through the clasp ring before closing (see Learn to Scoop on page 28).

3 With a new large ring, double the ring from Step 2.

4 With a new large ring, scoop 19 enameled copper rings, and go through the 3 previously added enameled copper rings. Close the large ring.

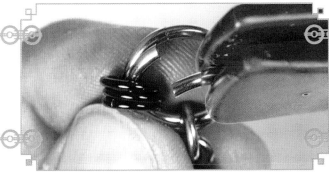

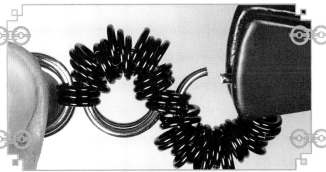

5 Double the last ring you added: This is a tight squeeze, so make sure your ring is open as narrowly as possible.

6 With a new large ring, scoop 19 enameled copper rings, and go through the final 3 enameled copper rings from the previous unit. Close the large ring.

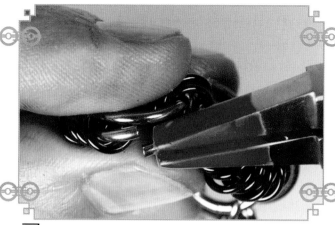

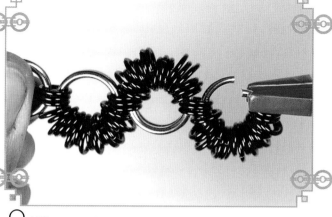

7 As before, double the large ring with a new large ring and close. If you have trouble closing the doubled ring, then you should add fewer than 19 enameled copper rings when you add new large rings. You can go back and add more after you've doubled the large rings.

8 With a new large ring, scoop 19 enameled copper rings, and go through the final 3 enameled copper rings from the previous unit. Before closing, make sure you're trapping the hanging rings on the opposite side of the weave from the first unit. Double this ring and close.

9 Continue the pattern of scooping 19 and trapping the previous rings on the opposite side of the weave until your necklace is the length you desire. On the last set of large rings, add only 3 hanging rings, to match the start of the weave.

10 To finish your piece, add a new large ring through the final 3 enameled copper rings and add the other side of the clasp (attach the remaining small brass rings to the clasp first). Double this large ring, just as you've doubled all the other large rings throughout the piece.

NOTE ABOUT RING SIZES

As with many of the coiled patterns, this weave is possible with a diverse number of ring sizes. You can adjust the coiled rings smaller or larger; thicker or thinner to achieve different effects. You can also adjust the size of the doubled large rings. Try a combination of size Z16—16 gauge, 15/32" (11.9mm) copper with H18—18 gauge, 3/16" (4.8mm) anodized aluminum.

CARING FOR COILS

When you pick up this weave after storing it, there may be one or two kinks at the joints of the tripled connector rings. Gently bend the weave back and forth at that point until the kink pops out of place.

Basic Coiled Choker Variation

Coiled DNA Bracelet

advanced · *Epic*

MATERIALS LIST FOR A 7 ¼" (18.4CM) BRACELET

26 large jump rings: P16 sterling silver—16 gauge, 5/16" (7.9mm)

426 small jump rings: D20 anodized niobium —20 gauge, 1/8" (3.2mm)

213 teal color blend

213 pink color blend

2 medium clasp rings: F17 sterling—17 gauge, 5/32" (4.0mm)

2–4 tiny clasp rings: D17 sterling silver—17 gauge, 1/8" (3.2mm)

toggle clasp

TOOLS

2–4 pairs of flat-nose pliers (2 pairs should have very thin jaws)

BASE METAL RING SUBSTITUTIONS

Large rings: P18—18 gauge, 5/16" (7.9mm)

Small rings: D20—20 gauge, 1/8" (3.2mm)

Take the basic coiled pattern one step further by using two colors. Each color swirls and overlaps forming a double helix motif. This bracelet is without a doubt one of the most impressive and meticulous chain mail patterns I've ever worked.

WEAVE IN A NUTSHELL

With a large ring, scoop as many tiny rings as you can and weave through the previous 3 tiny rings (make sure to alternate colors). Double that ring.

Continue adding tiny rings scooped on large rings; alternate colors on the sides of the weave, plus alternate the colors of the 3-Connectors you pass through.

Fill in the blank spaces with as many tiny rings as you can, matching the color of the surrounding rings.

Coiled Ring

 *advanced*

MATERIALS LIST

1 large jump ring: L18 stainless steel—18 gauge, 1/4" (6.4mm)

32–40 small jump rings: B22 anodized titanium—22 gauge, 3/32" (2.4mm) *The rings used in this project are hand cut and have a slightly different appearance than the rings used in other projects.*

12–27 tiny jump rings: C20 stainless steel—20 gauge, 7/64" (2.8mm)

7–10 stainless steel jump rings in sizes F18 (18 gauge, 5/32" [4.0mm]) to I18 (18 gauge, 13/64" [5.2mm]) (see Ring Sizing on page 60)

TOOLS

2 pairs of flat-nose pliers

This fun pattern is a best seller at jewelry shows. It is always one of the pieces that folks point to and gasp, "Oh, wow! Look at that! I had no idea chain mail could do that!" The pattern is simple, but steel and titanium are some of the most difficult-to-work-with rings, hence the advanced rating for this project.

1 Close approximately 20 of the anodized titanium rings and all of the tiny stainless steel rings. Open the remaining rings (see Closing Jump Rings on pages 20–25 and Opening Jump Rings on pages 26–27).

Scoop the closed titanium rings onto the large stainless steel ring and close the large ring (see Learn to Scoop on page 28). If it's difficult for you to close the large ring, let a few of the titanium rings drop off the large ring before closing it (you'll add them later).

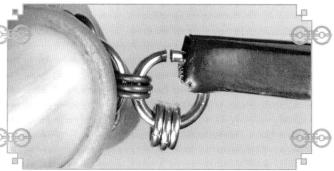

2 With a new 18 gauge stainless steel ring, scoop up 3 tiny stainless steel rings and weave through 3 of the titanium rings and close (see Closing Tough Rings on page 25).

3 Repeat Step 2 on the other side of the weave. There should be roughly the same number of titanium hanging rings on each side, but you don't need to count them yet.

4 Add new titanium rings on each side of the weave until you've squeezed in as many as possible, with equal numbers on each side. You should try to fill in at least 12 on each side, but you may be able to squeeze in up to 14 or more on each side.

5 Lengthen the band by scooping 3 new tiny rings with an 18 gauge stainless steel ring and weaving through the 3 stainless rings from Step 2.

Continue lengthening the band until it will fit snugly—but not tightly—around the appropriate finger. When you're adding the final ring, do not add any tiny rings.

6 Instead, bring the other part of the weave up to meet the final ring, and weave the ring through the 3 tiny rings from Step 3, closing the band.

Coiled X-Lock Byzantine Bracelet

 *intermediate*

One of the easiest coiled projects, this bracelet nonetheless is an attention-getter. The perfect combination of ring sizes causes the coiled rings to flare out, accentuating the X shape and adding a splash of brilliant color.

Mid-length project

MATERIALS LIST FOR A 7 ¾" (19.7CM) BRACELET

FOR THE X-LOCK

32 thin large jump rings: L18 jewelry brass—18 gauge, 1/4" (6.4mm)

8 thick medium jump rings: K16 jewelry brass—16 gauge, 15/64" (6.0mm)

32 small jump rings: F18 anodized aluminum, color red—18 gauge, 5/32" (4.0mm)

14 small jump rings: F18 jewelry brass—18 gauge, 5/32" (4.0mm)

4–6 tiny clasp rings: D18 jewelry brass—18 gauge, 1/8" (3.2mm)

toggle clasp

FOR THE COILING

48 small jump rings: F19 enameled copper, color orange—19 gauge, 5/32" (4.0mm)

TOOLS

2 pairs of flat-nose pliers

PRECIOUS METAL RING SUBSTITUTIONS

Use the ring sizes on page 86 for the X-Lock Byzantine portion of the weave, and add enameled copper rings in size F19 —19 gauge, 5/32"(4.0mm) for the coiling.

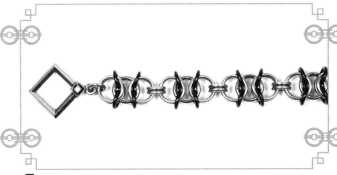

1 Open all the coiling rings, and prepare the X-Lock rings as instructed in the *X-Lock Byzantine Bracelet* on pages 86–89.

Create an *X-Lock Byzantine Bracelet* using the red anodized rings for the X shape.

2 Start to add the coiled edging by weaving an orange jump ring onto the first thick jewelry brass ring.

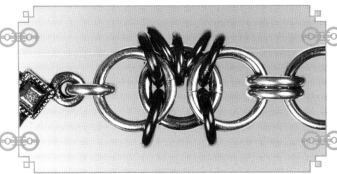

3 Add a second orange ring next to the first. Before adding the third, push down the second orange ring, so you create enough space to add the final ring. Add the third ring, then verify that the middle ring hangs lowest, and the first and third orange rings flare outward.

4 Repeat Steps 2-3 on the other side of the thick ring. When you're ready to add the third ring, it may appear as though there is not enough space. You may need to open the third orange ring slightly wider than normal, and position the leading edge of the ring in the right spot (even if it's hard to see the opening in the weave). Wiggle your way through, like a mole burrowing through a hole, and the ring should pop out on the other side of the weave. Close the ring.

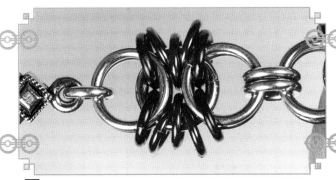

5 Verify that both sets of coiled rings are in the proper location—with the middle ring pushed in, and the outer rings flared out.

Repeat Steps 2–5 for the remaining thick rings.

Try varying the color of both the X-Lock rings and the coiling rings for different looks!

Coiled Helm Chain Bracelet

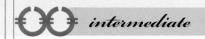

 *Long project*

MATERIALS LIST FOR A 7½" (19CM) BRACELET

FOR THE HELM CHAIN

40 large jump rings: N18 aluminum—18 gauge, 9/32" (7.1mm)

28 medium jump rings: H18 anodized aluminum, color black—18 gauge, 3/16" (4.8mm)

4 medium jump rings: H18 jewelry brass—18 gauge, 3/16" (4.8mm)

2–4 small jump rings: D18 jewelry brass—18 gauge, 1/8" (3.2mm)

toggle clasp

FOR THE COILING

156–182 small jump rings: F20 anodized aluminum, color gold—20 gauge, 5/32" (4.0mm)

168 tiny jump rings: D20 anodized aluminum, color gold—20 gauge, 1/8" (3.2mm)

TOOLS

2–4 pairs of flat-nose pliers (2 pairs should have very thin jaws)

PRECIOUS METAL RING SUBSTITUTIONS

Helm Chain

N16—16 gauge, 9/32" (7.1mm)

H17—17 gauge, 3/16" (4.8mm)

Coiling

F20—20 gauge, 5/32" (4.0mm)

D20—20 gauge, 1/8" (3.2mm)

Black rings march boldly down the center of the weave, framed by more than 300 gold edging rings to create Helm chain as you've never seen it before. From afar, no one would guess that this is chain mail.

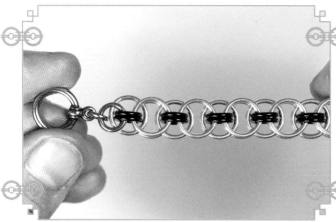

1 Follow the *Helm Chain Necklace* pattern on pages 97–98 to create the base of your bracelet. For this piece, I've finished the ends with brass rings because they match the coiled rings in color. However, you can finish with aluminum rings should you wish.

2 Start the coiling on the first set of large doubled aluminum rings. Begin to add small anodized rings onto one side of the weave, making sure to weave through both aluminum rings.

3 Add a total of 6 or 7 rings to the doubled rings. I find I can add 7 to some units, but not to all, so I scatter the 7-ring coils throughout the bracelet. You may even be able to squeeze in 8 (or more) rings as shown here depending on your ring size, but I suggest starting with 6 or 7 to ensure a balanced design. Push down on the outer coiled rings so that they sit against the single rings from the Helm base. This causes the inner coiled rings to be pushed upward.

4 Begin to add new small rings on the other side of the doubled large rings. Periodically you may need to use thin-jawed pliers to pull out 1 of the inner rings so that only the outer rings are pushed downward, which gives you more space to add new rings.

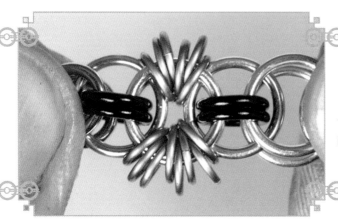

5 Add as many rings as you can to this side. Here, I've squeezed in 6. (Refer to the tip on the following page.)

You may need to open the last few rings in each coiled set wider than normal in order to get them through the weave without weaving them through neighboring coiled rings.

6 Move back 1 unit to the first single large Helm ring, and begin to add tiny rings to this ring. Note that we didn't start by coiling this ring because the tiny rings would spin around the single ring, potentially getting lodged between the doubled large rings. By filling in the doubled rings first, the new tiny rings we're adding will stay in their proper spots.

7 Try to squeeze 6 tiny rings onto the single large ring. Once again, make sure to push down the outer rings in the coiled set.

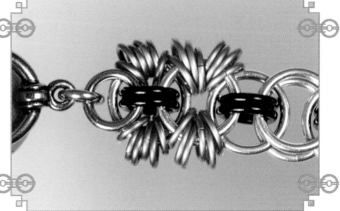

8 Repeat on the other side of the single large ring.

9 Now move to the next set of doubled Helm rings, and repeat Steps 3-4 for that set. Don't forget to switch back to adding small rings instead of tiny rings! Before moving on, verify that the outer coiled rings are pushed downward.

10 Add tiny rings to the single Helm ring in between the 2 coiled units.

11 Continue the pattern of adding small rings to the doubled Helm rings, then moving back to add tiny rings to the single Helm rings until the entire Helm edging has been added. Do not add any rings to the brass rings.

Try using 2 or even more colors for the coiling rings like I did in the bracelet above.

Coiled Japanese Lace Bracelet

 expert

 *Epic*

MATERIALS LIST FOR A 7¼" (18.4CM) BRACELET

FOR THE JAPANESE LACE

76 large jump rings: H18 aluminum—18 gauge, 3/16" (4.8mm)

154 tiny jump rings: D20 enameled copper, color lime—20 gauge, 1/8" (3.2mm)

12–14 small jump rings: D18 aluminum—18 gauge, 1/8" (3.2mm)

toggle clasp

FOR THE COILING

310 tiny jump rings: D20 enameled copper, color red—20 gauge, 1/8" (3.2mm)

TOOLS

2–4 pairs of flat-nose pliers (2 pairs should have very thin jaws)

PRECIOUS METAL RING SUBSTITUTIONS

H17—17 gauge, 3/16" (4.8mm)

D20—20 gauge, 1/8" (3.2mm)

From a distance, this bracelet resembles intricate beadwork. Use two contrasting colors for a striking effect. The dense texture—approximately seventy-two rings per inch—is one of the most tactilely satisfying patterns I've ever encountered. Be prepared for all your friends to exclaim, "Ooooh! Can I touch?"

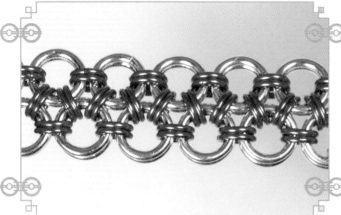

1 Open the large and tiny aluminum rings and 2 of the lime enameled copper rings. Close the remaining lime enameled copper rings and open all the red enameled copper rings (see Closing Jump Rings on pages 20–25 and Opening Jump Rings on pages 26–27). (Advanced students may choose to close some of the red enameled copper rings, too; see the tip on this page and Step 8.)

Follow the pattern for the *Reversible Japanese Lace Bracelet* on page 53–55 to create a 2-row bracelet. However, note that for this coiled version, the "large" rings are smaller than for the regular lace pattern.

2 To taper the ends, weave a new small aluminum jump ring through 4 of the hanging rings at the end, 2 from each row. Close the ring.

Tip

If you're advanced and your plier jaws are thin enough, you might be able to add a few coiled rings—raw or closed—as you weave the original Lace pattern (see Step 8).

3 Double the ring you just added.

4 Add a new lime ring to the 2 rings you added in Steps 2–3. Do not double this ring.

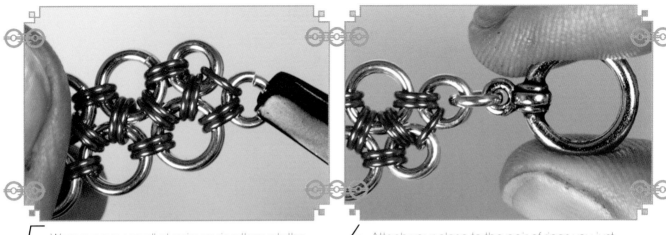

5 Weave a new small aluminum ring through the lime ring you just added as well as 2 hanging rings from the other row. Close the ring and double it.

6 Attach your clasp to the pair of rings you just added. Repeat on the other side of the weave.

7 Begin to add the red rings to each set of doubled rings in the Japanese Lace pattern.

8 Don't worry about adding the same number of rings to each set. You'll go back and fill them all in to full capacity soon enough!

9 Begin to add additional rings so that there are 8 red rings on each set of large rings. When you go back to add more coiled rings, you might need to open the final ring quite wide in order to guide it through.

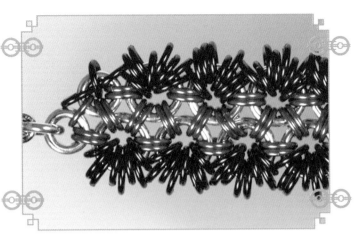

10 Add 3 red rings to the small set you added in Steps 2-3. Do not add any rings to the final small set that connects to the clasp.

The Coiled Japanese Lace pattern looks good in many different color combinations, but contrasting colors, like red and green or purple and yellow, are my favorites.

Coiled Japanese Diamond Pendant

For this variation, create a *Japanese Diamond Pendant* as shown on page 59, then coil the edges. For the larger jewelry brass pendant shown below right, use size P16—16 gauge, 5/16" (7.9mm) and F18—18 gauge, 5/32" (4.0mm) rings for the Japanese diamond and coiling.

Glossary

American Wire Gauge (AWG): A numbering system that is traditionally used for nonferrous (meaning not containing iron) metals. It's always best to ask your suppliers directly about the exact stats on their rings. All the precious metal rings in this book—sterling silver, gold-fill, niobium and titanium—are AWG. All the 20 gauge and 22 gauge base metal rings are also AWG.

Anodized: An anodized metal is one that has been electrically treated. By dipping niobium or titanium in an electrically charged solution, an oxide layer is formed and the surface color changes. The colors achieved depend on the voltage. When aluminum is anodized, the oxide layer is clear, and the metal is then dyed. Whether the colors are electrically obtained or dyed, the colors may vary from batch to batch and from ring to ring.

Aspect Ratio: The relationship between the Inner Diameter and the Wire Diameter of the ring. The formula to calculate AR is ID ÷ WD. High AR rings have a big hole with comparatively thin wire. You can fit a lot of similar jump rings through the hole of a high AR ring, so many weaves are possible, but most are far too loose to be aesthetically pleasing. Low AR rings have a small hole with comparatively thick wire. You can't fit a lot of rings through the center, so not many weaves are possible.

Base Metal: Normally a base metal is a metal that oxidizes or corrodes easily. In this book, for ease of grouping the non-precious metals into a cohesive group, base metal refers to aluminum, bronze, copper, enameled copper, jewelry brass and stainless steel.

Calipers: A tool to measure the ID, WD and OD of jump rings.

Double (a ring): When instructions call for you to double a ring, it means you need to add a ring of exactly the same size right next to the original ring. The doubled ring passes through exactly the same rings as the first ring. Some rings will be tripled in the same way.

Inner Diameter (ID): Refers to the inside "hole" of a jump ring. Typically given in millimeters or fractional inches. Best measured using calipers (to account for springback) when the jump ring is closed.

Jump Ring: This is where it all starts—the basic ring from which traditional mail is created.

Kerf: The width of cut made by a saw through a jump ring. Thick saws yield rings with large kerfs, and thin saws create rings with minimal kerfs. Smaller kerfs are better because the jump ring maintains more of its circular shape when closed if less metal is removed.

Leading Edge (of the ring): The end of the jump ring that will pass through the weave first. Each jump ring has two ends. You'll grip one side of the jump ring with your pliers (generally speaking, this will be the right side for right-handers, and the left side for left-handers). The edge of the ring on the opposite side is the leading edge.

Mandrel: A rod around which wire is coiled in order to make jump rings. The standard ring mandrels used for this book increase in 1/64" (0.4mm) increments.

Outer Diameter (OD): The outside measurement of a jump ring, from one end to another. Traditionally given in millimeters or decimal inches. Best measured using calipers when a jump ring is closed. Mail purists never give ring sizes in OD; however, bead supply companies often use OD to measure jump rings, since they are accustomed to measuring beads in OD.

Precious Metal: Precious metals are rare and of high economic value. This book considers precious metals to be gold-fill, sterling silver, niobium and titanium.

Raw Rings: Untouched jump rings, straight from the pack. Some weavers, like myself, prefer to add raw rings to a weave, and close the rings as we go, rather than opening and closing rings before weaving.

Saw-Cut: The name given to rings that are cut with a saw. These rings are generally considered preferable to machine- or pinch-cut rings for jewelry making. When closed properly, they are seamless. (The edges of machine- and pinch-cut rings are angled and therefore do not close flush.)

Springback: When raw wire is wrapped around a mandrel, it "relaxes" a bit after being coiled because it prefers to stay as a straight piece of wire. This relaxing is known as springback. Different metals have different springback. For example, a stainless steel jump ring wrapped around a 5/16" (7.9mm) mandrel is significantly larger than a copper ring wrapped around the same mandrel. This is because steel is tougher, and it springs back more. The same metal in different gauges wrapped around the same mandrel will yield different IDs, because springback differs depending on the gauge. Even within a metal, different tempers cause varied springback. Note also that different suppliers have different methods of wrapping, resulting in different springbacks even if the wire gauge and metal are the same. Springback affects aspect ratio, so be sure to take springback into account when ordering rings.

Standard Wire Gauge (SWG): Also known as Imperial Wire Gauge, this numbering system is often used for ferrous (meaning containing iron) metals. Stainless steel usually has SWG numbers. It's always best to ask your suppliers directly about the exact stats on their rings. All the base metals in this book—aluminum, copper, jewelry brass, bronze, stainless steel, enameled copper and anodized aluminum—are SWG for gauges 18 and thicker.

Temper: The hardness or softness of wire. Softer wire is more malleable, and harder wire is stiffer and more durable. Typical tempers include Dead Soft, Half Hard and Full Hard.

Weave: (noun) A specific pattern of jump rings. Weaves are divided into various families. (verb) The act of linking jump rings together into a pattern.

Wire Diameter (WD): The measured thickness of the wire used in a jump ring. Most commonly given in gauges, but since gauges are inconsistent (see Wire Gauge, AWG and SWG), many chain mailers prefer to give WD in millimeters or decimal inches.

Wire Gauge (g, ga, or gu): Gauges are numbers designating the thickness of the wire used to make the jump ring. Gauge systems differ according to the metal—16 gauge steel is different from 16 gauge sterling silver (see AWG and SWG). The main thing to remember about gauges is that the higher the number, the thinner the wire. Most armor chain mail is 12 gauge–16 gauge. Jewelry tends to be 16 gauge–22 gauge. Micromail is 22 gauge–24 gauge—and even thinner, for the hard-core micromailers! See the gauge conversion chart in the Ring Measurements section on page 17 for gauge measurements and conversions.

Work-hardening: Also known as strain hardening, this is the process of strengthening metal by bending, hammering, rubbing or otherwise working with it. However, if you attempt to work-harden a piece too much, it will become brittle and can break. (Have you ever played with a twist-tie or paper clip, bending it over and over and over again? After a few bends, its resistance increases as it is work-hardened. However, if you keep bending, eventually it snaps in two.)

INNER DIAMETER

Letter	Mandrel	aka	Decimal	Millimeter
	1/64"	insanity	0.016"	0.397
	2/64"	1/32"	0.031"	0.794
	3/64"		0.047"	1.191
AAA	4/64"	1/16"	0.063"	1.588
AA	5/64"		0.078"	1.984
B	6/64"	3/32"	0.094"	2.381
C	7/64"		0.109"	2.778
D	8/64"	1/8"	0.125"	3.175
E	9/64"		0.141"	3.572
F	10/64"	5/32"	0.156"	3.969
G	11/64"		0.172"	4.366
H	12/64"	3/16"	0.188"	4.763
I	13/64"		0.203"	5.159
J	14/64"	7/32"	0.219"	5.556
K	15/64"		0.234"	5.953
L	16/64"	1/4"	0.250"	6.350
M	17/64"		0.266"	6.747
N	18/64"	9/32"	0.281"	7.144
O	19/64"		0.297"	7.541
P	20/64"	5/16"	0.313"	7.938
Q	21/64"		0.328"	8.334
R	22/64"	11/32"	0.344"	8.731
S	23/64"		0.359"	9.128
T	24/64"	3/8"	0.375"	9.525
U	25/64"		0.391"	9.922
V	26/64"	13/32"	0.406"	10.319
W	27/64"		0.422"	10.716
X	28/64"	7/16"	0.438"	11.113
Y	29/64"		0.453"	11.509
Z	30/64"	15/32"	0.469"	11.906
BB	31/64"		0.484"	12.303
CC	32/64"	1/2"	0.500"	12.700
DD	33/64"		0.516"	13.097
EE	34/64"	17/32"	0.531"	13.494
FF	35/64"		0.547"	13.891
GG	36/64"	9/16"	0.563"	14.288
HH	37/64"		0.578"	14.684
II	38/64"	19/32"	0.594"	15.081
JJ	39/64"		0.609"	15.478
KK	40/64"	5/8"	0.625"	15.900
LL	41/64"		0.641"	16.272

Letter	Mandrel	aka	Decimal	Millimeter
MM	42/64"	21/32"	0.656"	16.669
NN	43/64"		0.672"	17.066
OO	44/64"	11/16"	0.688"	17.463
PP	45/64"		0.703"	17.859
QQ	46/64"	23/32"	0.719"	18.256
RR	47/64"		0.734"	18.653
SS	48/64"	3/4"	0.750"	19.050
TT	49/64"		0.766"	19.447
UU	50/64"	25/32"	0.781"	19.844
VV	51/64"		0.797"	20.241
WW	52/64"	13/16"	0.813"	20.638
XX	53/64"		0.828"	21.034
YY	54/64"	27/32"	0.844"	21.431
ZZ	55/64"		0.859"	21.828
	56/64"	7/8"	0.875"	22.225
	57/64"		0.891"	22.622
	58/64"	29/32"	0.906"	23.019
	59/64"		0.922"	23.416
	60/64"	15/16"	0.938"	23.813
	61/64"		0.953"	24.209
	62/64"	31/32"	0.969"	24.606
	63/64"		0.984"	25.003
	64/64"	1"	1.000"	25.400

Letter = My shorthand abbreviation for the mandrel size

Mandrel = The size of the mandrel

aka = The reduced fractions are typically used in the mail world; for example, one would say 3/16" rather than 12/64"

Decimal = The inch measurement expressed as a decimal rather than a fraction. Listed here for math geeks, as well as those looking to calculate aspect ratios.

Millimeter = The millimeter equivalent of the mandrel size for the vast majority of the rest of the world, which uses the metric system. Note that this chart lists sizes not included in this book, simply to give you a good bird's-eye view of potential sizes, and to more easily see how millimeter sizes correspond with the fractional inch sizes.

ASPECT RATIO
BASE METALS
All metals, unless otherwise noted

Gauge	Listing	AR
20	B20	3.1
20	C20	3.6
20	D20	4
20	E20	4.6
20	F20	5.1
20	G20	5.8
20	H20	6.2
20	I20	6.7
18	D18	2.8
18	E18	3.1
18	F18	3.6
18	G18	3.9
18	H18	4.1
18	I18	4.5
18	J18	5
18	K18	5.2
18	L18	5.6
18	N18	6.2
18	O18	6.6
18	P18	6.9
18	R18	7.8
18	T18	8.5
16	K16	4
16	L16	4.4
16	P16	5.4
16	T16	6.5
16	Z16	8.2
14	T14	5
12	X12	4.9

More information regarding inner diameter, aspect ratio and wire gauge can be found on pages 16–17.

ALUMINUM
20 gauge aluminum is generally available in a thinner wire than other metals, hence the higher aspect ratios. I've tried to include projects that aren't affected by this variance, allowing you to substitute copper for aluminum, and vice versa.

Gauge	Listing	AR
20	B20	3.3
20	C20	4
20	D20	4.6
20	E20	5.2
20	F20	5.8
20	G20	6.3
20	H20	6.9
20	I20	7.4

ENAMELED COPPER

Gauge	Listing	AR
20	D20	4
19	F19	3.8
19	H19	4.7

NIOBIUM

Gauge	Listing	AR
20	B20	3.1
20	D20	4.4
20	F20	5.4
18	F18	4.1
18	H18	5

PRECIOUS METALS
All metals, unless otherwise noted

Gauge	Listing	AR
21	B21	3.3
21	D21	4.6
20	B20	3
20	D20	4
20	E20	4.6
20	F20	5.3
19	D19	3.6
19	E19	4.2
19	G19	5.2
19	I19	6
18	E18	3.7
18	F18	4.1
18	H18	5
18	K18	6.3
17	D17	2.9
17	F17	3.6
17	G17	4
17	H17	4.3
17	J17	5.2
17	L17	5.9
17	P17	7.4
17	T17	8.9
16	F16	3.2
16	N16	6
16	O16	6.3
16	P16	6.6
15	K15	4.3
15	P15	5.9
14	J14	3.6
14	O14	4.9
14	S14	6
14	T14	6.4
12	T12	5.1
10	Z10	4.9
10	KK10	6.6

ANODIZED TITANIUM

Gauge	Listing	AR
22	B22	4.3

Some helpful articles about AR can be found at:
www.bluebuddhaboutique.com/resources/newsletter/2008/08-02.php
www.bluebuddhaboutique.com/resources/newsletter/2008/08-03.php
and
www.bluebuddhaboutique.com/faq/3_ProjectHelp.php

Recommended Suppliers & Resources

JUMP RINGS AND CHAIN MAIL SUPPLIES

BLUE BUDDHA BOUTIQUE
Chicago, Illinois
www.BlueBuddhaBoutique.com
(866) 602-RING (7464)
orders@bluebuddhaboutique.com
Kits and supplies to make every project in this book, plus countless other chain mail supplies.

C&T DESIGNS
www.candtdesigns.com
support@candtdesigns.com
(719) 337-6131
A U.S.-based chain mail manufacturing and supply company. A wide array of metals and sizes, including shaped wire. Custom sizes on request.

METAL DESIGNZ
www.metaldesignz.com
sales@metaldesignz.com
Manufactures the highest quality saw-cut jump rings in many different metals.

SPIDERCHAIN JEWELRY
www.spiderchain.com
Precision-cut jump rings in a zillion sizes—specializing in precious metals.

CLASPS AND FINDINGS

C-KOOP BEADS
www.ckoopbeads.com
sara@ckoopbeads.com
(218) 525-7333
C-Koop Beads has been making enameled beads, buttons and components for the past ten years. Each piece is a little piece of art.

SAKI SILVER
www.sakisilver.com
Highly textured and dramatic clasps, pendants and findings in sterling silver, gold-fill, shibuichi and bronze.

BEADS AND GENERAL JEWELRY SUPPLIES

RIO GRANDE
Albuquerque, New Mexico
www.riogrande.com
(800) 545-6566

YOUR LOCAL BEAD STORE
Support local businesses! Write in the contact information for your favorite bead shops below, so you'll always have it handy.

_____

_____

_____

_____

_____

_____

ONLINE CHAIN MAIL RESOURCES

M.A.I.L.—MAILLE ARTISANS INTERNATIONAL LEAGUE
www.mailleartisans.org

THE MAIL RESEARCH SOCIETY (FOR HISTORICAL INFORMATION)
www.themailresearchsociety.erikds.com/

An up-to-date listing of more resources, including other suppliers' and chain mail artists' Web sites, can be found on the Blue Buddha Boutique website www.bluebuddhaboutique.com/resources

Index

Find more inspiration with these books

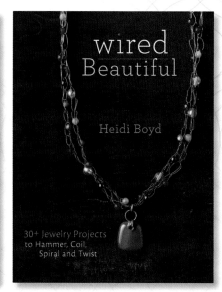

Add a romantic twist to your creative time with *Beaded Allure*. Inside you'll find projects and techniques to give your beadweaving the soft and romantic aesthetic you've always dreamed of. Author Kelly Wiese will lead you through the ins and outs of a variety of stitches, and you'll use those stitches in 25 stepped-out projects.

paperback; 8.25" × 10.875"; 144 pages
ISBN-10: 1-60061-768-9
ISBN-13: 978-1-60061-768-3
SRN: Z4956

Learn to approach color as a painter does—your palette will be rainbow-hued beads, and your paintings will be spectacular jewelry! *Beaded Colorways* includes in-depth discussions about color theory—accompanied by color wheels—that are then used to show you how to mix beads and gems together to create custom color blends called Bead Soups. These "soups" are then woven together into dazzling pieces that are more like works of art than simple jewelry.

paperback; 8.25" × 10.875"; 128 pages
ISBN-10: 1-60061-318-7
ISBN-13: 978-1-60061-318-0
SRN: Z2925

Wired Beautiful features more than 30 projects and a complete basic techniques section that will have you excited about the numerous ways of using wire in your jewelry projects. Best-selling author Heidi Boyd brings her sensible instruction and beautiful design skills to wire jewelry. Learn the ins and outs of working with wire for jewelry designs and enjoy the fresh design approach and great techniques. Each chapter includes step-by-step photos and expert instruction for each project, as well as inspirational variations.

paperback; 8.25" × 10.875"; 128 pages
ISBN-10: 1-4403-0310-X
ISBN-13: 978-1-4403-0310-4
SRN: Z6886

These and other fine North Light titles are available at your local craft retailer, bookstore or online supplier, or visit our website at www.mycraftivitystore.com.